# Reversing the Tao: A Framework for Credible Space Deterrence

# Reversing the Tao: A Framework for Credible Space Deterrence

*Madison!*
*Victorium Per Astra!*
*Best of Luck!*

**Christopher M Stone**

ISBN: 1533276137
ISBN 13: 9781533276131

# Acknowledgements

This book originally began as my master's thesis at the Department of Defense and Strategic Studies, Missouri State University. As a result, there are many I must acknowledge for helping me get through this project with such a stellar product. A sincere thank you to my thesis committee, Dr. Dana Johnson, Dr. Kerry Kartchner, and Dr. Peppino DeBiaso for their professional guidance and mentoring through this process. To Col M.V. "Coyote" Smith, USAF (PhD), and Maj Brent Ziarnick, USAFR (PhD) for their friendship and support of this and other spacepower writing projects. Thank you also to Peter Marquez, former Director of Space Policy, National Security Council, Dean Cheng, Dr. Jim Vedda, Dr. Pete Hays, the OSD Office of Net Assessment, my colleagues at the Principal DoD Space Advisor Staff Policy and Integration Division and finally, but not least, to my parents Michael and Linda Stone and my beautiful wife Barbra Stone for their support over the years of my pursuit of a career in national security, space and strategy and to God for sovereignly merging the three into my career reality. This work is dedicated to my beautiful daughter Katherine Diane Stone. May she grow up in the traditional American way of life preserved and secured through American spacepower.

# Table of Contents

# List of Tables

# List of Figures

# Preface

The use of space has led to tremendous advancements in humanity's quality of life. The list of these advancements is well known and oft repeated. Space provides services that modern society cannot function without. But space is not a sovereign nation nor does it have its own interests. Space is utilized by people and by countries that have their own needs and interests. Yet, there has been a movement to protect space from hostilities through a "one-size fits all" deterrence theory for the space environment.

But deterrence theory and practice has never been about changing an environment- it is about keeping an actor from doing something you do not want them to do. In the Cold War the U.S. did not deter missiles, the U.S. deterred the Soviet Union from using those missiles against the U.S. and its allies. For deterrence to be successful you have to understand the other actor's desires and their pain points. You have to develop and maintain the capabilities to deny any benefits the actor would gain by attacking you and also have the demonstrated desire and capability to impose costs on the actor should deterrence fail.

In the following work, Chris Stone does an excellent job deconstructing the current Department of Defense policy on space deterrence, explains the threats and motivations of China, and provides a tailored path forward for developing a true deterrent capability focused on an actor and not a place.

Peter Marquez
Former Director of Space Policy (2007-2010)
U.S. National Security Council
April 2016

# Foreword

*Adversaries are developing kinetic, directed-energy, and cyber tools to deny, degrade, and destroy our space capabilities... They understand our reliance on space, and they understand the competitive advantage we derive from space. The need for vigilance has never been greater.*
—GENERAL JOHN HYTEN, COMMANDER
AIR FORCE SPACE COMMAND, MARCH 2016

I n this book Christopher Stone welcomes readers to the age of space warfare. It is a welcome that is long overdue because—all rhetoric aside—space was never a sanctuary. Predictably, counter-space weapons evolved almost as quickly as artificial satellites themselves. Nuclear weapons were tested in space in the 1960s and kinetic impacting anti-satellite weapons were tested in the following years. However, such weapons demonstrated indiscriminant second and third order effects that curtail their military utility. Novices in the field of space security continue to discuss such weapons while real space warfare has been going unnoticed. Decades of jamming, lasing, and other directed energy attacks against satellites or the signals they carry, precede this book. Such attacks have become commonplace in both war and peace, but no one talks about them.

The deafening silence about space warfare comes from four sources. First, conservatives never like sharing information about space attacks because they fear doing so may expose vulnerabilities that adversaries could exploit later.

Second, liberals persist in propagating the sanctuary myth because they fear disclosing information about space attacks will entice more actors to develop their own counter-space programs. Third, commercial satellite operators remain quiet because they fear losing money if their customers lose confidence in their ability to assure services. Finally, members of the arms control community, who mean well, but whose valiant attempts to put the genie back in the bottle through treaties, codes of conduct, and rules of the road have failed, but they fear the situation will worsen if they concede defeat.

As a result, some diplomats and think tank wonks attempt to define away the problem. In their minds, as long as there is no bloodshed or property damage, such attacks fail to meet their criteria of violence. Without violence they assert that such attacks are not acts of war. They dismiss attacks in cyberspace this way as well. Accordingly, they insist that the attacked party has no right to respond to attacks with military force either in space or elsewhere. Instead, they claim the attacked party should redress their grievances in the courts. Unfortunately, the courts neither deter attacks, nor defend targeted satellites or their signals. Attackers take great care to avoid detection, frustrate the attribution process, and otherwise medal with the evidentiary trail in ways that make the courts ineffective tools to redress losses in space warfare. In sum, satellite operators and users are on their own in the face of increasing attacks. Frustration is mounting, as indicated by the tone of General Hyten's quotation that begins this foreword.

Over the last several administrations, the United States has evolved towards what could be called a "soft" deterrence policy in space. Within its National Space Policies and National Security Space Strategies it asserts the right to defend its satellites and states its intention to deter attacks though international partnerships and the use of commercial satellites carrying multi-national traffic. In other words, hiding in the crowd of multi-national non-combatants. While this might deter attackers from employing kinetically destructive weapons against whole satellites, it does not deter precision jamming, cyber, or other directed energy attacks against specific signals supporting military or economic traffic.

Attacks continue. The silence continues. One wonders if a new international norm has been established that non-kinetic attacks against satellites are an acceptable practice?

This is the backdrop against which this book was written.

In this work, Christopher Stone provides another method of putting the genie back in the bottle; deterrence the old fashioned way—in the tradition of peace through strength. Readers will enjoy the review of classic deterrence theory that he provides. They will also discover herein a refreshing exercise of comparing and contrasting the traditional deterrence model to the "peace through mutual vulnerability" concept that guides western policies today.

Be warned: readers need to engage his arguments introspectively. At issue is an examination not only of human nature, but of political and cultural behavior as well. He points out that westerners are often guilty of mirror imaging. That is the fallacy of assuming that our values of life, liberty, and the pursuit of happiness are shared uniformly among all peoples around the globe. They are not. Many of us carry scares that prove this.

I commend this book to all readers, especially those interested in space policy, deterrence theory, and strategy. This book is not the last word on the subject of space deterrence, but it is one of the first. Stone takes a stand. Most do not. He will be pilloried by those who deny or dismiss the current state of space warfare because that is the politically correct thing to do, and quite often it pays.

Among my fellow Space Weapons Officers, Chris Stone finds a comfortable home. We are curious and welcome the intellectual challenge offered here. We watch politics unfold up close and with our lives on the line. Some tell us that ours is not to reason why. Oh, but it is.

Kudos to Christopher Stone for daring to write this book! Ad Astra!

M.V. "Coyote" Smith, Colonel, USAF (PhD)
Professor of Strategic Space Studies
Montgomery, Alabama

# Introduction

In the foreword to Roberta Wohlstetter's book *Pearl Harbor: Warning and Decision*, Thomas Schelling stated that "there is a tendency in our planning to confuse the unfamiliar with the improbable. The contingency we have not considered looks strange; what looks strange is thought improbable; what is improbable need not be considered seriously."[1] In the arena of the strategic space environment, this lesson of the past seems to have been lost on the creators of the present DoD space deterrence concept found in the 2011 Secretary of Defense/Director of National Intelligence's National Security Space Strategy (NSSS) as many of the threats deemed improbable by commentators and researchers within this topic have become policy while US space systems, critical infrastructure in their own right upon which the American system of economics, defense and diplomacy are dependent, remain vulnerable to a surprise attack on the order and magnitude of the 1941 Pearl Harbor attack.

This book will examine this space deterrence concept and the ideological foundations as compared with classical deterrence theory, modern deterrence theory, and potential adversary strategic culture. The potential adversary analyzed will be the People's Republic of China as its rapid development and advancement of counterspace forces have raised the concern of many in the national security space community and highlights the importance of evaluating and observing strategic culture and behavior of the adversary to understand

---

1 Wholstetter, Roberta. <u>Pearl Harbor: Warning and Decision</u>. Stanford University Press. 1962. P. vii

the trends found in strategic reality rather than expecting national leaders to accept American concepts without the context of where they are situated in geography and thought. Deterrence without understanding the decision cycle of the adversary will not be effective.

Chapter 1 will begin by analyzing the four elements of the NSSS space deterrence through the prism of history with the deterrence theories of Herman Kahn, Thomas Schelling, and Keith Payne. These three were chosen as representatives of the various deterrence theories throughout Cold War and post-Cold War history. This review of the development of deterrence theory in the Western world will demonstrate that while the word "deterrence" is utilized in the NSSS, the DoD space deterrence concept is not, in fact, deterrence at all.

Chapter 2 highlights the unique strategic culture and worldview of the Chinese people and their government as devised and led by the Chinese Communist Party (CCP) and its influence upon their views of space doctrine, warfighting capabilities and deterrence definitions. This chapter will provide analysis that demonstrates why the NSSS is not deterring this potential near peer adversary due to the drafters' apparent lack of understanding of the Chinese unique strategic culture and ignoring of their objectives and behavior in favor of an ineffective plan.

Chapter 3 provides further details of what is at stake in this discussion on space deterrence and the importance of the United States to prepare for the potential for destructive warfighting within the space domain. It utilizes a combination of Chinese strategic thinking with the theories of John Boyd and Herman Kahn[2] to develop a way to achieve an escalation dominance within a tiered, tailored approach to deterrence in space consisting of a near term achievable triad of capabilities. These capabilities provide near term, achievable active defenses and deterrent capacity to reverse the first strike instability inherent in the strategic environment due to the NSSS' ineffective deterrent strategy.

---

2 During the analysis found in Chapter 1 and 2 on the state of deterrence views from both a Western and Chinese perspective, Herman Kahn's approach to having a robust set of capabilities (offensive and defensive) appears to have more application to a war that extends or begins in space over the Pacific with the Chinese. In addition, as Chapter 2 and 3 will highlight, Col John Boyd's analysis and proposals for rapid decision making and deterrence synchronize well with the merger of Chinese thought and American spacepower force application at the strategic and operational levels.

This book's objective is to provide an appraisal of what is considered improbable to highlight that history and experience have shown that those actions that some in the government and academia view as improbable are the result of mirror imaging. Furthermore, such improbabilities could very well lead the US into a situation where American and allied way of life is severely damaged by a surprise attack that will be as one author put it, "not due to a lack of warning, but the result of a tendency to dismiss as reckless what we consider improbable."[3] The United States must prepare for what is improbable to some, to protect the homeland and its vital interests.

---

3 Rumsfeld, Donald et al. <u>Report of the Commission to Assess United States National Security Space Management and Organization</u>.2001.p. 15

# CHAPTER 1

## Security Through Vulnerability: The National Security Space Strategy's View of Space Deterrence

> *"Culture is at the root and foundation of strategy"*
> *- PEOPLE'S LIBERATION ARMY (PLA) GENERAL LI JIJUN*

> *"A nation's security cannot be based solely on estimations of its [adversary's] military capacity"*
> *DR. BARRY SCHNEIDER, TAILORED DETERRENCE*

The concept of deterrence has been an integral part of American national security strategy for decades. Following a debris-generating Chinese anti-satellite (ASAT) test in 2007, some in the space policy community began to question whether or not the space domain was destined to become a theater of warfare and if its days as a sanctuary[4] free from weaponization were over.[5] Since then the world has witnessed several more non-destructive ASAT tests by the Chinese, lasing of satellites, and an apparent new norm

---

4 The Arms Control Association has referred to weapons in space as a "radical and reckless option" and that any country that flight-tests, deploys or uses space weapons is a threat to the activities of all other space faring nations.

5 Some authors such as Lt Col Bruce DeBlois have argued over the last several years that space sanctuary has been the best national policy to protect our advantages. However, space has not been a sanctuary given his own admission of Soviet co-orbital ASATs being tested and deployed from the late 1960s until the end of the Cold War. Sanctuary must mean all weapons, not just US weapons. Sadly, it appears his definition only applies to US weapons. See "Space Sanctuary: A Viable National Strategy, Air and Space Power Journal Winter 1998

of nation-state behavior[6] in space via the tripling of reversible counterspace attacks such as jamming and other means of interference.[7] This increased counterspace activity creates fear in the minds of some space arms control advocates that any conflict that includes space will result in leaving low Earth orbit unusable and "endangering all those who operate" in space.[8]

Due to these and other concerns, numerous organizations began in 2009 to research the possibility of utilizing a strategy of deterrence as an answer to the threat of the proliferation of space weapons and the likelihood of their use in anger. This chapter will examine the National Security Space Strategy's (NSSS) concept of space deterrence through a historical lens comparing and contrasting its four elements of space deterrence with the nuclear deterrence theories of Herman Kahn, Thomas Schelling, and post-Cold War theorists such as Keith Payne.

## An Overview of the NSSS's Four Elements Deterrent Effects

There have been several space deterrence concepts proposed since 2008, but only one has become formal DoD strategy: the "delicate balance of risk"[9] or four elements concept.[10] Originally devised by the Eisenhower Center for Space and Defense Studies at the US Air Force Academy in 2010, it was adopted by the Office of Secretary of Defense's Space Policy office then under the leadership of Ambassador Gregory Schulte in 2011[11]. The vision of this

---

6 A norm of behavior is defined by Michael Krepon as standards of proper or acceptable behavior - See more at: http://spacenews.com/41789norm-setting-for-outer-space/#sthash.hH9NIG5D.dpuf

7 De Selding, Peter B. "Eutelsat Blames Ethiopia as Jamming Incidents Triple". Space News. June 6, 2014

8 Weeden, Brian et al. An Introduction to Ostrom's Eighth Principles for Sustainable Governance of Common-Pool Resources as a Possible Framework for Sustainable Governance of Space. 2010

9 Harrison, et al. "The Delicate Balance of Risk": Space Deterrence Study. Eisenhower Center for Space and Defense Studies. USAFA. 2010

10 Those space deterrence theories include: Forrest Morgan's "First Strike Stability in Space", Brian Weeden's "Denial Deterrence" and the Eisenhower Center for Space and Defense's "A Stable Balance of Risk"-four elements

11 Ambassador Gregory Schulte was a career diplomat with an emphasis on arms control negotiation prior to his assignment as Deputy Assistant Secretary of Defense for Space Policy.

concept as codified in the NSSS is to "dissuade and deter the development, testing, and employment of counterspace systems and prevent and deter aggression against space systems and supporting infrastructure that support US national security."[12]

The NSSS's multi-layered concept consists of 1) Deterrence Through Norms;2) Deterrence Through Entanglement/Alliances; 3) Deterrence Through Resilience; and 4) Deterrence Through Response.[13] Below is a short synopsis of each of these elements.

In the first element, the DoD states that a "top down diplomatic initiative"[14] that promotes the "responsible use of space"[15] and condemns the "activities that threaten the safety, stability and security of the space domain"[16] will "preserve our advantage"[17] in space as well as deter potential aggressors from interfering or attacking United States and allied space systems. According to Ambassador Schulte, the deterrent effect of this element of space deterrence is through the process of defining what is and is not responsible behavior.[18] Examples of this process include the European Union-proposed International Code of Conduct as well as the advancement of transparency and confidence building measures (TCBMs).[19] Enforcement of these norms could occur through the diplomatic and economic isolation of irresponsible actors should any states deviate from the agreed, yet legally non-binding framework. International pressures based on non-legally

---

12  National Security Space Strategy. 2011

13  Harrison et al. "The Delicate Balance of Risk": Space Deterrence Study. Eisenhower Center for Space and Defense Studies. USAFA. 2010

14  Schulte, Gregory. "Protecting Global Security in Space". Presentation at the S. Rajaratnam School of International Studies Nanyang Technological University, Singapore, May 9, 2012

15  National Security Space Strategy. Department of Defense. 2011. P. 2

16  Ibid. P. 2

17  Schulte et. al. "Enhancing Security Through Responsible Use of Space." Strategic Studies Quarterly. 2011.

18  Schulte, Gregory. "Protecting Global Security in Space". Presentation at the S. Rajaratnam School of International Studies Nanyang Technological University, Singapore, May 9, 2012 p. 5

19  Ibid. p. 11

binding agreements are the tools of deterrence through norms according to the present DoD strategy.[20]

The second element discussed in the NSSS is "Deterrence Through Entanglement," specifically, the development of "alliances with other space faring nations...and international organizations."[21] The idea is if an adversary nation, not deterred by the agreed, non-legally binding norms of responsible behavior, decides to act in a destabilizing manner by attacking or interfering with a US or allied spacecraft, the fact that those spacecraft have the backing and reliance of multiple nation states would make it less likely that the adversary would strike.[22] These alliances, it should be noted, are about the sharing of satellite services. No evidence is provided to indicate that any active space defenses or retaliatory terrestrial options are included in such alliance relationships from either the United States or with US allies and space partners. The cooperative agreements between the United States and Australia with the Wideband Global SATCOM satellites (WGS) is one example of this type of relationship.[23]

As a result of the lack of counterspace capabilities through the alliances, the responses could be economic or diplomatic in nature, or perhaps least likely, lead to some unstated terrestrial military response. However, despite this lack of stated enforcement or protection capacity of the alliances proposed, it is stated in speeches and articles that this construct will "alter the enemy's targeting calculus" and create in the mind of an adversary nation some restraint of attacking several nations rather than just one.[24]

The third element is described as "deterrence through resilience." This measure would assure "cost-effective protection" of US space systems supporting both conventional and nuclear command and control through measures

---

20 Author's note: Using all instruments of national power is the preferred method, what is different is the reliance on only a few and a heavy emphasis on an uncoordinated and hollow perceived diplomatic framework.

21 National Security Space Strategy. Department of Defense. 2011. P.3

22 Schulte, Gregory. "Protecting Global Security in Space". Presentation at the S. Rajaratnam School of International Studies Nanyang Technological University, Singapore May 9, 2012. P.5

23 Ibid. p. 5

24 One paper refers to this concept as a "100 Satellite Deterrent" speaking of sharing constellations of vital capabilities but with no mention of how to defend these satellites upon which more nations are now reliant.

such as the improvement of our "intelligence posture" via space situational awareness capabilities and "disaggregation." [25] These capabilities enable the United States to "better monitor and attribute activities in the space domain [and] maintain awareness of ...the capabilities, activities and intentions of others."[26] The resilience concept of disaggregation requires that, rather than building large, single mission architectures of a few satellites, changing the architecture to include smaller, dispersed satellites or hosting payloads on civil or commercial spacecraft would create a means to maintain some operational capability following an attack, thereby denying benefit of the attack to the adversary[27]. As Air Force Space Command's 2013 White Paper on the topic states: "Disaggregation is an innovative opportunity to stay ahead of our adversaries, to change their targeting calculus, and to mitigate the effects of a widespread attack on our space assets. In addition, resilience serves as a deterrent, which may be the best way to preserve our capability by avoiding an attack."[28]

Finally, there is the fourth deterrent element, which is labeled "deterrence through response." As the NSSS states, this deterrent is to follow after an attack has taken place and shows that the United States "retains the right and capabilities to respond in self-defense, should deterrence fail."[29] These responses, however will "not necessarily come from space," creating some uncertainty as to what, if anything, the United States would do in the event of space deterrence failure. As noted earlier, the NSSS does not specifically go into any details about what type of capabilities, active defenses, or offensive retaliatory strike options either terrestrially or in space are required to assure either the US or the allies of the credibility of the deterrent effect of the this response option in the NSSS. In addition, there appears to be some disconnect between this DoD strategy and

---

25  "Resiliency and Disaggregated Space Architectures." Air Force Space Command White Paper. 2013. P. 12

26  National Security Space Strategy. Department of Defense. P. 17

27  Disaggregation is defined by Air Force Space Command as: the dispersion of space-based missions, functions or sensors across multiple systems spanning one or more orbital plane, platform, host or domain.

28  "Resiliency and Disaggregated Space Architectures." Air Force Space Command White Paper. 2013. P. 10

29  National Security Space Strategy. Department of Defense. P.17

the National Space Policy of the United States of America released by the White House in 2010. In the latter document, it states that the United States will "deter others from interference and attack, defend our space systems and contribute to the defense of allied space systems, and, if deterrence fails, defeat efforts to attack them."[30]

## The Space Deterrence of the National Security Space Strategy: Its Ideological Foundations

Defending space systems is critical due to the strategic and force multiplier effects derived from them.[31] However, as one commentator wrote, "Recently posited theories of space deterrence misuse the term deterrence, they do not grasp the intent of deterrence, the full range of other security constructs, and, most importantly, what should be done when, not if, deterrence fails."[32] Looking at the NSSS' concept of space deterrence through the historical lens of classical deterrence theory highlights his point. This then begs the question, if this concept does not grasp the intent of deterrence, why was the four element concept adopted?

Deterrence, according to DoD doctrine is defined as: "The prevention of action by the existence of a credible threat of unacceptable counteraction and/ or belief that the cost of action outweighs the perceived benefits."[33] Merriam-Webster defines deterrence, in the context of politics, as "the policy of developing a lot of military power so that other countries will not attack your country."[34] The action that the United States aimed to prevent throughout the Cold War through "a lot of military power" was a surprise nuclear attack

30  White House, National Space Policy of the United States of America. June 2010. P. 3
31  Marquez, Peter. "Space Deterrence: The Pret a Porter Suit for the Naked Emperor." Marshall Institute. 2011. P.9
32  Ibid. p 9
33  JP 1-02 Dictionary of Military Terms
34  Merriam-Webster Dictionary Online. www.merriam-webster.com

by the Soviet Union, or a nuclear Pearl Harbor as the Surprise Attack Panel[35] referred to it.[36]

As stated above, the common threat being deterred is hostile acts in space and their resulting impacts on the "sustainability of outer space."[37] However, as with the idealist arms control position of the Cold War nuclear policy debate, the mere presence of nuclear weapons was considered the common threat. Likewise, the idealists promoting arms control as a space deterrence concept consider the presence of weapons in space in a similar manner and the threats posed by near peer adversaries, such as China's multi-layered capabilities, less of an issue than space debris.[38] This is supported by the overarching vision of the NSSS.

As an example, within Schelling's stable balance of terror concept of nuclear deterrence, each side maintains a survivable, similar, deterrent force capable of quick retaliation if attacked. The space deterrence strategy in the NSSS does not advocate for a second strike option, much less a first-strike option, in the event of deterrence failure. The strategy rejects the testing, deployment, and use of space weapons as being destabilizing to the sustainability of outer space and its use for peaceful purposes. The deterrence of the "delicate balance of risk" is predicated on the belief that, like the idealist view of international relations, security and deterrence in space can be achieved through the international system and institutions, such as treaties and codes of conduct. Thus, deterrent effect is not based on any overt threat

---

35 Terrill, Delbert R. The Air Force Role in Developing International Outer Space Law. AU Press. p. 8

36 The Surprise Attack Panel was a group of government and industry leaders who were tasked with assessing the vulnerability of the United States to a surprise nuclear strike by the Soviet Union in the early days of the Cold War. The goal was to prevent a nuclear Pearl Harbor, through the development of an adequate national defense infrastructure coupled with robust intelligence to prevent surprise.

37 The 2013 Space Security Index states, "The application of some destructive negation capabilities, such as kinetic-intercept vehicles, would also generate space debris that could potentially inflict widespread damage on other space systems and undermine the sustainability of outer space." The report is managed and published by Project Ploughshares with support and funding from Secure World Foundation, The Simons Foundation, the International Security Research and Outreach Programme at Foreign Affairs and International Trade Canada, and the Erin J.C. Arsenault Trust at McGill University. See http://ploughshares.ca/ t

38 Michael Krepon has been quoted in editorials in Space News as saying that the Earth is surrounded by thousands of space weapons in the form of orbital debris. .

of retaliation or the prevention of damage to space systems from attack through active defenses, but through the implied threat of isolation through the international community of nations. As defined earlier, this is not the traditional definition of deterrence.

## Analysis - Schelling, Kahn, and Post-Cold War Theories Meet the DoD Space Deterrence Strategy

The idea of space warfare, especially of kinetic engagements in orbital space is viewed by many as "unthinkable" given the aforementioned fear of a debris-laden "tragedy of the commons."[39] As with the Cold War decision to prevent nuclear war through deterrence rather than fight an "unthinkable" general war, so space deterrence seeks to avert the destabilizing actions of war extending into the space domain.

However, as part of the nuclear Cold War strategy, American policymakers believed that for effective deterrence of aggression from the Soviet Union, there needed to be a strong, survivable deterrent force ready and willing to retaliate. Schelling promoted an easy to understand and "cost effective" stable balance of terror model that agreed with this need for a strong, survivable deterrent. In addition, in order to prevent a "reciprocal fear of surprise attack," or in other words a fear that we would attack first, the creation of active defenses or counterforce capabilities would be prohibited. Schelling's theory was also reliant on the vulnerability of American cities to Soviet nuclear weapons. Some defenses were admissible in this concept. Schelling supported the defense of the deterrent force itself through passive means such as hardening and dispersal of forces that would thereby confuse "an enemy's targeting calculus."

From an arms control position, Schelling advocated for a stable balance of capability, rather than disarmament as the goal. Both societies being mutually vulnerable to attack was key to prevent the need for what was claimed to be destabilizing options such as ballistic missile defenses and first-strike weapons.

Herman Kahn's view of nuclear deterrence disagreed with Schelling's advocacy of a stable balance; rather, he believed that giving the President multiple capabilities and weapons platforms to retaliate with if deterrence failed,

---

39 Weeden, Brian et al. "An Introduction to Ostrom's Eight Principles for Sustainable Governance of Common-Pool Resources as a Possible Framework for Sustainable Governance in Space. IAC-13-E3.4.2. p. 3

was essential.[40] However, simply stating that you had a strong deterrent capability and you intended to use that force means nothing if it is not credible. To ensure credibility of the will to use that deterrent force, defenses to protect the American people were essential so that the Soviets understood that the Americans would keep their extended deterrence and homeland deterrence roles by not having to commit national suicide in the process of defending allies overseas. This would assure the Soviets that Americans would keep their commitments and would not be blackmailed by threats or acts of aggression.[41]

Strategic messaging was an important part of both Schelling and Kahn's deterrence theories. Schelling's stable balance of terror was designed to assure the Soviets of our second strike capability, while Kahn's credible deterrence concept was designed to assure allies relying on extended deterrence and the American people.[42]

When reviewing the aforementioned DoD space deterrent proposals, one can see that they use the term deterrence in a very different manner than those of Schelling and Kahn. As one commentator stated, "...they do not grasp the intent of deterrence, the full range of other security constructs and, most importantly, what should be done when, not if, deterrence fails."[43] In the arena of strategic messaging, the present DoD space deterrence strategy is, like Schelling's, meant more to assure potential adversaries of what we will not do, rather than what we will do. As an example, the NSSS states that by not developing ASAT weapons for active defense or offensive retaliatory forces, and continuing to promote responsible behavior through non-binding norms and TCBMs, we are ensuring protection and security of our space systems. In some ways, like Schelling, this idea appears to desire a sort of certainty of uncertainty[44] that while the United States has not articulated how or with what force it would defend itself, the United States reserves the right to

40 Payne, Keith. <u>The Great American Gamble</u>. National Institute for Public Policy Press. 2008. P. 51

41 Ibid. P. 52

42 Ibid. p. 52

43 Marquez, Peter. "Space Deterrence: The Pret a Porter Suit for the Naked Emperor". <u>Marshall Institute,</u> 2011

44 "Certainty of uncertainty" is a phrase Thomas Schelling in <u>Arms and Influence</u> use to describe that being certain that uncertainty exists regarding potential adversary retaliation enables deterrence to be effective.

act in self-defense. This type of uncertainty, however, is counter to both the Schelling and Kahn models as it lacks the explicit commitment to retaliate. The space deterrence concept in the NSSS is similar to Schelling's views in that it adheres to the belief that defenses of any kind, excluding measures to ensure survivability, are prohibited given the goal of the NSSS is to prevent the placement and use of weapons disrupting the sanctuary of orbital space.

Regarding the concept of deterrence through resilience, as during the Cold War when nuclear forces were dispersed globally and hardened to ensure survivability and the "confusing of the enemy's targeting calculus," so this concept of resilience aims to achieve a deterrent effect by a similar confusion of targeting in space. While disaggregation and other resilience measures promoted in the NSSS do offer some interesting concepts related to survivability, the NSSS does not provide any more deterrent effect or defense to space attack[45] than the dispersal of ICBMs did in preventing the development of nuclear counterforce weapons by the Soviet Union during the Cold War. These measures in the Cold War led to more weapons being built to threaten the US nuclear forces and society, not less creation or less testing of nuclear weapons. In the 21st Century strategic space environment, having more targets in space may challenge a potential adversary's targeting calculus, but given different national interests and strategic cultures, it may not deter its weapons testing.  It will more likely lead to more weapons or capabilities to defeat the disaggregated architectures and passive measures employed.

Despite the respect the concepts of Kahn and Schelling of Cold War deterrence theories have and the lessons that can be applied to space deterrence frameworks, the Post-Cold War deterrence theories (also known as Third Wave), such as those developed by Keith Payne, adds additional context to the discussion.[46] Unlike others, Payne believes that the Cold War

---

45 The DoD Nuclear Matters Handbook states that dispersing nuclear forces as part of survivability enhancement enhances both "deterrent value and the potential military utility" of nuclear forces but not deterrent effect.

46 The term "third wave" is used to describe post-Cold War deterrence theorists such as Keith Payne and Therese Delpech. These writers do not simply add to the thoughts of the past, in many cases they refute and replace the classical theory with new perspectives related to strategic culture and decisional intent rather than mirror imaged view of national leaders. Keith Payne has published such works as The Great American Gamble and The Fallacies of Cold War Deterrence, while Delpech has published such works as Nuclear Deterrence in the 21st Century. All are cited in this book.

frameworks were not as effective in the Cold War due to many factors. One of these factors was that both Schelling and Kahn relied on the idea that national leadership on both sides consisted of rational actors with similar concepts of cost and benefit. As Payne noted, "historical studies consistently demonstrate that the deterrence theory assumption of well-informed leaders operating reasonably, rationally, and thus predictably, frequently does not correspond with actual crisis decision making; and deterrence, therefore, can fail or not apply."[47] Thus, as with Cold War deterrence theory, the space deterrence theory of the NSSS is based on the assumption that national leaders are rational actors who will agree with the proposed norms of behavior and their definition of what is considered "responsible." Why is this not a realistic expectation? This is because of numerous factors such as "an individual's personal beliefs and characteristics, a leadership's political goals, ideology, perception of threat, [and] determination"[48] among other traits. A look at history highlights a recurring theme that "beliefs and modes of thought have been the dynamic behind some of the most significant and surprising decision making"[49] in the last century.

It appears that during the 2009-10 Space Posture Review's[50] development of these deterrent elements for space, there was a lack of robust historical analysis undertaken with respect to each element and whether or not, in other domains such as air, land or sea, these concepts have been effective in preventing war or use of certain types of weaponry[51]. Regarding the deterrence

---

47  Payne, Keith. <u>The Fallacies of Cold War Deterrence</u>. National Institute for Public Policy Press. p. 39

48  Ibid. p. 40

49  Ibid. p. 40

50  The Space Posture Review of 2009-10 was a congressionally mandated activity, tied to the development of the Quadrennial Defense Review (QDR) and the Ballistic Missile Defense Review (BMDR) to highlight to Congress the plan for how the DoD would prepare and posture space forces due to the development of counterspace capabilities with near-peer nations such as China. This was partially of interest due to the aftermath of the 2007 destructive Chinese ASAT test.

51  During my experience in the Space Posture Review, watching its implementation, reading the guiding documents, reading the classical theories of deterrence and interviewing senior American leaders across the government who were engaged in these discussions, it appears that there was a lack of understanding from a historical perspective, theoretical perspective and a strategic cultural perspective.

through norms element of the policy, there have been numerous occasions where treaties, conventions, and covenants between nations were breached. In fact, a look at the historical track record shows that the real norm of international relations is that of treaty or convention breach.[52] While it is a laudable goal to push for norms of non-interference in space, the reality of the space environment heralded in the open press highlights is that of reversible interference[53] at least, and the desire of kinetic ASATs and testing by many space faring nations at worst.[54]

One example of how the space deterrence framework has not taken into account the dynamics of political differences of leadership is related to the resilience/deterrence by denial concept. The NSSS stated that the space deterrence strategy following this model "doesn't need to be specifically created for a certain adversary in a certain situation… [and that one doesn't] need to know who the adversary is."[55] The document asserts that it works as a blanket strategy within the international system. This Schelling-type view suggests that many of the underlying assumptions of the DoD space deterrence strategy may be based on mirror imaging.[56] As Payne notes, "[S]pinning out untutored certitudes about how a foreign leadership sees the world and should behave is relatively easy and extreme confidence in deterrence in comforting…"[57] This is what the NSSS appears to be providing to the DoD as its strategy rather than confronting the issues in a realistic and achievable way.

Mirror imaging is a cognitive trap where planners or policymakers believe that their adversaries think like they do and share the same fears, beliefs, and worldview. Examples of mirror imaging within the four elements include the assumption that nations that do not accept the "norms of responsible

---

52 Beilenson, Laurence W. The Treaty Trap. Public Affairs Press.1969.

53 Reversible interference is a type of space attack where the effects generated against an adversary are not permanent or fully destructive but can be reversed and enable adversary spacecraft to resume normal operations.

54 De Selding, Peter B. "Eutelsat Blames Ethiopia as Jamming Incidents Triple." Space News. June 6, 2014

55 Weeden, Brian. "Protecting Space Assets through Denial Deterrence." Secure World Foundation Presentation. P. 24

56 Mirror imaging is defined as is "the analysts' assumption that the people being studied think like the analysts themselves" according to Laura Wittin of Johns Hopkins University

57 Payne, Keith. The Fallacies of Cold War Deterrence. Univ of Kentucky Press. p. 100

behavior" would agree they are acting "irresponsibly" as defined by the US Department of Defense, especially if it contradicts what they perceive as their vital national interests.

Despite the foundational principles of DoD space deterrence being within the space sanctuary and idealist school of international relations theory, the fact that the DoD NSSS advocates for new norms of responsible behavior and codes of conduct may indicate a realization that this foundation of space as a sanctuary is not reflective of reality and indicates an attempt to be perceived in the international arena as promoting the world they seek rather than the world that is.[58] In addition, the utilization of terminology such as "fight through" and "operate in degraded environments" highlights the failure of the objective of the NSSS's deterrence structures.[59]

Finally, the fourth element of this concept is "deterrence through response." Rather than providing a clear articulation of what, as one observer called "the willingness to use power to punish hostile actions," this strategy provides very broad and nebulous statements indicating a lack of will and capability to respond forcefully.[60] As stated recently, "China... [has] already developed counterspace capabilities and have shown the political willingness to use these weapons..."[61] However, the United States and its allies are not developing sets of military options to accompany the diplomatic options tailored for the types of adversaries we are likely to engage, or are already taking hits from on the reversible side. The vulnerability of our spacecraft, which are more and more becoming critical infrastructure for our economy and military

---

58 The 2010 National Security Strategy contained a section entitled "The World We Seek".

59 Air Force Space Command has used the phrase "fight through" or "operate in degraded environments" to refer to an ability to deny an adversary's impact by continuing forward with normal operations despite being seriously degraded by adversary actions. Both phrases have recently been applied to OSD Space Policy's recent document on "resiliency" entitled "Space Domain Mission Assurance: A Resilience Taxonomy" where this concept is defined further as "The ability of an architecture to support the functions necessary for mission success with... shorter periods of reduced capability...in spite of hostile action or adverse conditions.." in other words, deterrence failed but we are denying success of the adversary despite the facts to the contrary.

60 Marquez, Peter. "Space Deterrence: The Pret a Porter Suit for the Naked Emperor". Marshall Institute.2011.p.11

61 Ibid. p. 13

force projection, is not a security policy or one of effective deterrence. In fact, it could be perceived as an invitation to strike.

## Chapter Conclusions

The NSSS' space deterrence strategy provides a construct that while well intentioned, lacks a firm understanding of the lessons from Cold War deterrence and the contextual understanding of the security environments in terms of historical and cultural realties raised by the post-Cold War nuclear deterrence advocates. The four elements approach to deterrence appears to be an incomplete strategy focused heavily on a perceived diplomatic framework for the promotion of an arms control agenda in support of the sanctuary spacepower theory, not the deterrence of aggression and the active protection of United States access to and freedom of action in space. It lacks the robust strategic cultural, historical, and psychological substance necessary to create a framework needed to deter or dissuade the use of space weapons of either a reversible or more permanent nature.

The fact that states have increasingly been conducting reversible space attacks against other states and private sector space owners and operators over the years has shown that the real norm of behavior in space between states is of interference, not non-interference. The active ASAT testing highlights that NSSS is not deterring the testing and development of space weapons systems as the NSSS asserts it does. While engaging in the promotion of resilience, the ability to absorb attacks and have redundancies are good first steps, other nations are engaging in more aggressive efforts to develop and deploy active space offensive and defensive capabilities. We are only deterring ourselves with our own sophistry which fails to pass the reality check.

To paraphrase Therese Delpech, self-deterrence encourages the proliferation of space weapons, and it may become an invitation to actually use them.[62] We must re-look at the space deterrence concept the DoD is using to create our future architectures and strategies for space security, so we are better able to tailor our deterrence strategy to the adversaries we might face and are facing in the strategic environment of space.

---

62  Delpech, Therese. <u>Nuclear Deterrence in the 21<sup>st</sup> Century</u>. RAND. 2012

The United States, through the DoD/DNI's space deterrence concept in the National Security Space Strategy, is not effectively deterring potential near peer adversaries such as the People's Republic of China. This is partially due to a lack of understanding of the importance of strategic culture in assessing the intent of adversary leadership during peacetime escalation to crisis to effective deter further escalation to war. As a result, the present space deterrence concept lacks familiarity with classical deterrence thought as well as the critical differences between Western and Eastern concepts of deterrence. This will be covered in detail in Chapter 2.

# CHAPTER 2

## The Implications of Chinese Strategic Culture on Chinese Counter-Intervention and Space Deterrence Operations

> *"Anti-satellite weapons can be developed at low cost and that can strike at the enemy's enormously expensive yet vulnerable space systems will become an important option...to deter...powerful enemies...."-*
> PLA Analysts Li Hechun and Chen Youong *"Sky War – A New form of War That Might Erupt in the Future,"*
> *Liberation Army Daily (online), 17 January 2001*

> *"Strategic thought is always formed on the basis of certain historical and national cultural traditions, and formulation and performance of strategy by strategists are always controlled and driven by certain cultural ideology and historical cultural complex"*
> *-PLA's The Science of Military Strategy 2005*

The People's Republic of China (PRC) and its rapidly evolving space forces are viewed to be one of the principal threats to the United States' national security space infrastructure and the US capability for timely force projection in the Pacific Theater[63]. This view, especially given the 2007

---

63  Pollpeter, Kevin. China Dream, Space Dream: A Report Prepared for the U.S.-China Economic and Security Commission. IGCC. 2014.p. 11

kinetic ASAT weapons test, added emphasis to the Space Posture Review of 2010 and the Department of Defense's quest for deterrence as a means to secure the sanctuary of space from weaponization. This chapter will examine the strategic culture of the PRC and how it impacts the space deterrence philosophies of both the PRC and the United States Department of Defense.

## A Brief History of Mirror Imaging in DoD Deterrence Policy

The United States has typically been very effective at assessing adversary capabilities using overhead reconnaissance technology and other capabilities to develop assessments on adversary orders of battle and force laydown. However, a much more difficult task is assessing an adversary's intent[64]. This important facet of getting the "big picture" is essentially finding an answer to that "why" question behind an adversary's decision calculus and resulting strategic actions.[65] Understanding the rationale behind a nation's cost/benefit worldview is important for effective deterrence. As Sun Tzu wrote, it is better to win the battle in the mind of the enemy commander before the battle begins than during an actual engagement.[66]

The assumption of a deterrence environment between two rational, stable governments with similar views on cost/benefit analysis has been proven throughout history to be much less realistic. [67] In addition, relying on assumptions of adversaries being deterred by a gentleman's agreement, treaty, or code of conduct alone fails to recognize the historical record of such an approach to national security and deterrence.[68] During the Cold War, it was widely

---

64  Elder, Robert. From the Head to the Feet. Air University Press. 2011

65  As General Robert Elder, USAF (Ret.) said, "using technology and intelligence expertise developed over many years, we [the United States] do a relatively good job estimating adversary capabilities; we are not nearly as good at estimating the intent of state...actors." From the Head to the Feet, p. xv

66  Sun Tzu. The Art of War. Shambhala Dragon Edition. Boston. 1988. p.67

67  Keith B. Payne states in his work Fallacies of Cold War Deterrence that confidence in the belief that challengers will reliably observe agreed upon norms, "recognize and believe US demonstrations of will, understand the situation, calculate rationally, and then be deterred is an inadequate basis upon which to establish American security..." page 31

68  Laurence W. Beilenson states in his classic work on the history of international treaties and conventions, The Treaty Trap, that the historical record of peace treaties and other international compacts has been that of breach and non-compliance, rather than continued compliance and peace.

viewed as the foundation of deterrence that an adversary would be rational and reasonable and therefore predictable and controllable.[69] As a result of this worldview, American theorists viewed both sides within a nuclear deterrence construct as having devastating capability to retaliate under a "mutual restraint" structure as the best approach for enhancing "stability" and "security." [70] This "mutual vulnerability" model would keep the world safe as any rational leader would be deterred from aggression by the threat of prompt second strike by the other side.

Payne argues that this methodology was "taken to the extreme in the United States" through the minimal attention given to the "specific thoughts, goals and values of the Soviet leadership" and that many scholars and policymakers "assumed that they knew how any 'sane' Soviet leader would view nuclear weapons, and how deterrence would therefore operate."[71] In reality, nobody really knew the prospective damage that was needed to effectively deter the Soviet leadership and therefore "[United States] values and norms [were] ascribed to the Soviet leadership" driving U.S. conclusions and planning on how to deter the Soviet Union.[72] This "mirror imaging," while easy to grasp and more comforting than a full analysis of adversary values, norms, and decision making processes, led to the perpetuation of the fallacy that this concept of "mutual deterrence" was in fact "stable" and effective in protecting the US and allied populations and strategic interests. Evidence shown after the end of the Cold War highlights the "lethal mismatch between Western deterrence theory and Soviet war planning," that may have led to serious repercussions had any crisis escalated.[73]

This same type of mirror imaging has, unfortunately, served as the model of development for the DoD's space deterrence framework codified in the NSSS. Congressional hearings, speeches, and strategy journal articles by then-Deputy Assistant Secretary of Defense for Space Policy, Ambassador Gregory Schulte, and others in the Office of the Secretary of Defense highlight this "mutual vulnerability" view as the baseline for the DoD's present space

69 Payne, Keith. op. cit.,. p. 17

70 Gompert, David C. "Mutual Restraint in Space", Paradox of Power: Sino-American Strategic Restraint in an Age of Vulnerability. National Defense University.2011. p. 112

71 Payne p. 19

72 Payne p. 19

73 Ibid. p. 23

deterrence framework. In his presentation to the US-China Economic and Security Commission in 2011, Ambassador Schulte stated that while China was developing a vast array of counterspace capabilities and tested kinetic intercept anti-satellite (ASAT) weapons, the Chinese government "shares our interest in the safety, stability, and security of the [space] domain"[74] and "have common interests in promoting the peaceful use of outer space."[75] In addition, Schulte stressed the importance of the "common understanding of the operating domain" between the US and China and how "increasing the transparency of space operations" reduces the risk of miscalculation in a future crisis. [76]

Does the People's Republic of China truly share the same security interests in space with the United States? Does the Chinese government have common interests in space with respect to reducing the risks of miscalculation through increased transparency of space operations? Can the DoD leadership rely on its view of space deterrence to deter or dissuade the Chinese from the "development, testing, and employment of counterspace systems," much less preventing and deterring "aggression against space systems and supporting infrastructure"?[77] The answer to the latter question can be found through an assessment of the Chinese leadership's thoughts, goals and values by examining Chinese strategic culture and its influence on [Chinese] [the People's Liberation Army's] space deterrence and warfighting doctrines for the space domain.[78]

---

74 Schulte, Gregory. "China and the New National Security Space Strategy". A Presentation to the U.S.-China Economic and Security Review Commission. May 11, 2011. P. 4

75 Ibid. p. 4

76 Ibid. p.

77 Secretary of Defense and Director of National Intelligence, <u>National Security Space Strategy</u>. Department of Defense and Office of the Director of National Intelligence. 2011. P. 10

78 Everett Dolman in his book *Astropolitik: Classical Geopolitics in the Space Age*, provides a realist summary of the push for international norms: "The rhetoric of harmony and cooperation that attends most popular accounts of humanity's entry into outer space simply belies the historical record. Despite an ongoing effort to make the cosmos an international commons (the so-called "province of mankind", expansion into near-Earth space came not as the accommodating effort of many nations joined as one, but rather as an integral component of an overall strategy applied by wary superstates attempting to ensure their political survival... They established an international regime that ensured none of them could obtained an unanticipated advantage in space domination-for if any one nation did, the face of international politics might be changed forever." This has been the goal of arms control conventions since Russia hosted the first Hague Convention in the late 19th century.

## The Chinese Strategic Culture and Its Tao of Space Deterrence

Historians and scholars consider China to be one of the oldest civilizations in the world, lasting for over 5000 years. Many observers of China's interaction with other nations throughout history refer to it as "a civilization pretending to be a nation-state."[79] In Chinese mythology, this civilization is said to have no beginning. As one example, when the Yellow Emperor, considered the founding hero of China, came to power, it was seen as a restoration of the Chinese empire, not the beginning.[80] For most of the subsequent several thousand years, "the central goal of China's [imperial] security strategy had been defending the economic, political, social, and cultural heartland of China from invasion from…populations and kingdoms residing along China's periphery"-in short, maintaining its territorial integrity.[81] According to Chinese scholars, "the ancient Chinese Dynasties that ruled for millennia over China placed great emphasis on eliminating these "barbarian" threats-not through …military action [alone], but rather through peaceful diplomatic means."[82] In the 1998 Chinese Defense White Paper, the Chinese government references this traditional belief of cultural superiority-based self-defense when it states, "The defensive nature of China's national defense policy…springs from the country's historical and cultural traditions… China is a country with 5000 years of civilization, and a peace-loving tradition. Ancient Chinese thinkers advocated 'associating with benevolent gentlemen and befriending good neighbors' which shows that throughout history the Chinese people have longed for peace in the world and for relations of friendship with the people of other countries."[83]

The Chinese view of the world has been shaped by history and the blending of three different philosophies: Taoism, Confucianism, and much later Buddhism. Each of these emphasized harmony and discouraged abstract speculation or friction.[84] In these philosophies, the world is constantly changing

---

79 Kissinger, Henry. <u>On China</u>. Penguin Book. 2011. P.1

80 Ibid. p. 5

81 Richardson, Derek. <u>The Rise of the Dualistic Dragon: Contrastive Strategic Mentality of the People's Republic of China Under American Hegemonism</u>. Univ. of Victoria. 2008. Pp. 16

82 Ibid. p. 16

83 Ibid. p. 16

84 Nisbett, Richard. <u>The Geography of Thought: How Asians and Westerners Think Differently and Why.</u> Free Press. New York. 2003.p. 12

and is full of contradictions. To understand and appreciate one state of affairs requires the existence of its opposite; what seems to be true now may be the opposite of what it really is. In contrast to Western perspectives of linear paths of cause and effect within international relations, Confucianism (meaning the tradition of the scholars) was "the mainstream intellectual and ethical tradition in China."[85] Chinese Confucian based thinking tends to view the world as an "organic whole, difficult to separate into parts, just as the various schools of thought are often interrelated, in spite of...disagreements and conflicts."[86] Confucian writings view the Chinese hierarchical place in the international order as starting with the existence of a supreme and just Heaven, which oversees the world otherwise known as "all under Heaven: (tianxia). Heaven gives the mandate to rule the world to a worthy man and removes it from all tyrants, thereby allowing the use of armed rebellion and/or revolutions. This Mandate of Heaven [legitimizes all] authority including the authority of the [Chinese government's] right to pursue war."[87] Under the authority given by this Mandate, China is bestowed "the Middle Kingdom," or the "central country, status with total supremacy over the known world. [88] As a result of this Sinocentric worldview, China subsequently viewed the rest of the [nations] as living in "descending states of barbarism" the farther away they are from China's political and cultural frontiers."[89] This view of the world remained with the Chinese dynasties and governments until the beginning of the "century of humiliation" in the late nineteenth century.

In addition, Confucianism stresses economic well-being and education. The individual within the Chinese strategic culture works not for self-benefits but for the collective society. Therefore, the Western concept of liberty and individualism that Americans hold dear is alien to this culture.

---

85  Cheng, Julie. "Confucianism and WMD.: <u>Ethics and Weapons of Mass Destruction.</u> Cambridge Press. 2004. Pp. 248

86  Cheng, Julie. "Confucianism and WMD." <u>Ethics and Weapons of Mass Destruction.</u> Cambridge Press. 2004. P. 249

87  Ibid. p. 250

88  As Richard Nisbett stated in <u>The Geography of Thought</u>, the name of China in its native tongue means "the center."

89  Richardson, Derek. <u>The Rise of the Dualistic Dragon: Contrastive Strategic Mentality of the People's Republic of China Under American Hegemonism.</u> Univ. of Victoria. 2008. Pp. 19

To institutionalize the Chinese concept of world governance and cultural supremacy of the Chinese, a tributary system was created. This system was based on a hierarchical structure patterned on the Confucian notion of the "state" which was modeled after the concept of the family unit. [90] This hierarchical world order "utilized unequal relationships between China and its barbarian vassals, but this inequality was likened to that between father and sons in the Confucian family, unequal but benign."[91]

Rather than use military force to "eliminate and control barbarian threats and deter invasion, the Confucian tributary system "emphasized the sufficiency of the emperor's "virtue" to win the peaceful submission of men from afar without the employment of force or threats."[92] As Confucius wrote, "If remote people are rebellious [from the Sinocentric world order], our civil culture is to be cultivated to attract them to our virtues; and when they have been attracted, they must be made contented and tranquil...He who exercises the government by means of virtues may be compared to the north polar star, which keeps its place and all the stars turn towards it."[93] This is an example of "cultural moralism" whereby it is "better to win hearts and minds than to attack towns and cities."[94] Q. Edward Wang stated that "for some Confucian scholars, to cultivate moral principles and promote culture among non-Hans [non-Chinese] was more important than to subdue them with military victory... [and achieve] territorial gains."[95]

While Chinese leaders preferred this use of virtue to subdue the tributaries and other threats to its territorial integrity, the Confucian philosophy also "permitted the limited use of military means to restore Sinocentric order. Sun-Tzu understood this reality when he stated that there are times when even the most virtuous leader must resort to arms in order to maintain social and

90  Richardson, Derek. The Rise of the Dualistic Dragon: Contrastive Strategic Mentality of the People's Republic of China Under American Hegemonism. Univ. of Victoria. 2008. Pp. 20

91  Ibid. p. 20

92  Ibid. p. 20-21

93  Ibid. 21

94  Qing Cao, "Selling culture: ancient Chinese conceptions of 'the other' in legends," The Zen of International Relations: IR Theories from East to West, ed. S. Chan. Basingstoke & New York. 2001 p.8

95  Ibid. p. 21

political order."[96] One author quoted Yongjin Zhang on this Chinese responsibility "as the superior moral power...for maintaining and harmonizing this [Sinocentric] order with the moral examples it set, with institutional innovations and with force in maintaining Chinese dominance and control" within the "Mandate."[97]

Decisions to use force to restore the Mandate of Heaven and China's "centralized authority" are often "linked with the concept of 'just' or "righteous wars."[98] Andrew Scobell mentioned this when he connected the use of force to a Chinese "just war" doctrine: "The distinction is simple: just wars are good wars, and unjust wars are bad ones. Just wars are those fought by oppressed groups against oppressors, unjust wars are ones waged by oppressors against the oppressed. In contemporary Chinese Communist Party (CCP) thinking, China has long been internally viewed as a weak, oppressed country fighting against powerful imperialists. Thus for many Chinese, any war fought by their country is by definition a just conflict even a war in which China strikes first."[99]

When the British and other Western representatives arrived in China in the 1800s, some Chinese leaders believed that the many "centuries of predominance had warped the Celestial Court's sense of [strategic] reality."[100] Instead of relying on a tribute-based diplomatic presence backed by strong imperial military power, to protect their national and international interests, the Imperial leadership had devolved to a point where they maintained "no knowledge of armaments."[101] As a result, the British fleet arrived to enforce terms of trade through coercive military power and diplomacy through what are referred to by the CCP as "unequal treaties" leading to the "century of humiliation."[102] As Henry Kissinger said about the arrival of the British, "... the Europeans did not view [their activities] as conquest at all. They were not seeking to replace the existing dynasty--they simply imposed an entirely new world order essentially incompatible with the Chinese one." At the same time,

---

96  Ibid. p. 39
97  Ibid. p. 31
98  Ibid p. 32
99  Scobell, Andrew. China and Strategic Culture. Strategic Studies Institute. 2002. P.11
100  Ibid. p. 49
101  Ibid. p. 49
102  Ibid. p. 49

"an expansionist and military dominant Russia sought to pry loose China's vast hinterland [from the north and west]..." Russia, like the Europeans, had no desire to claim the "Mandate of Heaven" from the Qing rulers, but to achieve their East Asian security and strategic objectives. However, the Japanese, "[did not have a] vested interest in the survival of Chinese ancient institutions or the Sino-centric world order. From the east it set out not only to occupy significant portions of Chinese territory, but to supplant Beijing as the center of a new East Asian international order."[103]

Due to the lack of strength within the Middle Kingdom, then led by the Qing government, the "century of humiliation" became the rallying cry that future leaders of the People's Republic of China seized upon to ensure that China would never be perceived weak again and would do whatever it took to restore itself to its "rightful place" as the keeper of peace and harmony in world order. To do this required a stronger military force, the embracing of new economic models "with Chinese characteristics" as well as investments in science and technology as the keys to progress and the advancement of Chinese values. Today, vestiges of the Confucian principles of protecting and restoring the territorial integrity of China are still ever present in the CCP plans and strategies. This desire to achieve strength and the "rightful place" of China in the international hierarchy of nations leads to the present Chinese nature which is more aggressive in nature, including the use of strong military power cloaked in the aura of self-defense and the promotion of peace in the Asia-Pacific region and beyond.

## Manifestations of Strategic Culture in Chinese Strategic Decision Calculus

When reviewing this historical development of the Chinese strategic culture one can see the importance of sovereignty, self-defense, territorial integrity and cultural superiority of strength to the Chinese government. These strategic cultural concepts mentioned earlier, such as sovereignty, and the Sino-centric worldview of territorial integrity have influenced CCP views of the United States, the space environment, space deterrence, and warfighting doctrines.

103 Richardson, Derek. The Rise of the Dualistic Dragon: Contrastive Strategic Mentality of the People's Republic of China Under American Hegemonism. University of Victoria. 2008 p.58

Given the present international order is based upon Western values, norms and moral principles, deterring the leadership of People's Republic of China in space and on Earth requires more than simply projecting "universal" norms upon them, expecting them to simply agree to it, and to cease all development and deployment of their space weapons programs. As seen above, the Chinese have a very unique worldview based on centuries of history, a fusion of philosophical/religious views of Sino-Centric harmony, collective identity instead of individual freedom and the importance of maintaining control through active defense, and the resolution of unsettled claims in the returning of China to its rightful place of dominance and power.

While the United States holds free agency and individual liberty to be central to its way of life and helped codify these principals within the United Nations Charter for centuries the Chinese were first and foremost members of a collective. This includes the clan, the village and especially the family.[104] The individual was not and is not presently viewed as an "encapsulated unit who maintained a unique identity, across social settings."[105] The Chinese counterpart to individual liberty is "harmony." As a member of a perceived harmonious society, as individuals the Chinese have been concerned less with issues of control of others or the environment than with self-control within this system so as to minimize "friction" with others in their family and village and to make it easier to obey the requirements of the state" regardless of the governmental form or political ideology.[106] The ideal of happiness within the present day Chinese Dream is not a life allowing the free exercise of distinctive talents, but the satisfaction of a plain country life shared within a harmonious society. Communist leader Mao Zedong tapped into this collective, harmonious identity in the 1930s and 1940s when he created the People's War concept and the PLA that executed the Party's wishes to eventually take control of the mainland and unify China once again. This plan still remains a priority to regain its rightful place as a world power and ensure the control of Chinese destiny to reclaim lost territories and gain influence through CCP expansionist objectives in the Pacific and

---

104 Nisbett, Richard. The Geography of Thought: How Asians and Westerners Think Differently and Why. Free Press. New York. 2003.p. 5

105 Ibid. p. 5

106 Ibid. p. 5

worldwide.[107]    As current Chinese President Xi Jinping has stated: "In the best of Chinese traditions, generations of overseas Chinese never forget their home country, their origins, or the blood of the Chinese nation flowing in their veins. They have given their enthusiastic support to China's revolution, construction and reform".[108]

This collective agency is an elaboration of a deeply rooted concept going back thousands of years, of the obligations that were maintained between the emperor and subject, parent and child, husband and wife, and older brother and younger brother. The Chinese cultural system, absorbs the individual into a large, complex society where these obligations are the guide to ethical conduct in the Sino-centric world. This type of view impacts the Chinese concept of offensive deterrence. The strategic reality of the Chinese view of the early 21st century space and terrestrial environments is as it has been for years: to the Chinese space strategist, and key CCP leaders, the world is constantly changing and is full of contradictions.[109] To the Chinese strategist, to understand and appreciate one state of affairs in complex strategic planning requires the existence of its opposite, what seems to be true now may be the opposite of what it seems to be.[110] Thus, this type of view is applicable to the strategic domain of space, when the Chinese sign onto international agreements such as the Outer Space Treaty (OST) when their strategic behavior appears to trend toward another course. As John Boyd stated, strategists must focus not on technology or capabilities assessments in a vacuum, they must recognize and follow strategic behavior.

Some examples of this include that Chinese legal authorities and methods of negotiation reserve the right to change their position or withdraw from treaties that many in the West view as eternal. They reserve the right to change, given that what was true in 1967 may not be true today or supportive for the goals and objectives of the China Dream. This China Dream, which

---

107 Tanner, Scott. China's Emerging National Security Interests and their Impact on the People's Liberation Army. Marine Corps University. 2015. P.21

108 Xi, Jinping. "The Rejuvenation of the Chines Nation is a Dream Shared by All Chinese". The Governance of China. 2015. P. 69

109 President Xi Jinping in his address of April 7, 2013, he quoted a proverb often repeated in other speeches, "A wise man changes his ways as circumstances change, a knowledgeable person alters his means as time evolves.

110 Nisbett, Richard. The Geography of Thought: How Asians and Westerners Think Differently and Why. Free Press. New York. 2003 p. 13

is the re-establishment of the Sino-Centric order, or in other words, harmony in place of the friction that dominates the United States led international system under the UN Charter.[111]Senior CCP leaders have repeatedly stated the importance of China's role in "building a harmonious world internationally" as the keepers of and propagators of harmony in the world.[112] Xi Jinping has stated numerous times that "every one of the 1.3 billion Chinese [are part of the team necessary] to disseminate Chinese morality and culture."[113]

In the Chinese view, the world moves in endless cycles, not a perpetual linearity leading to exponential growth and prosperity among equals in the international system. This complexity of the Chinese view is highlighted by the continued use of the Tao-or "the Way." While Confucianism stressed economic well-being for the collective order, the Tao blended with this philosophy to appreciate the contradictions and changes and the need to see things as a whole. This is integral to the notion of the perceived "yin-yang universe" which also complements the longstanding Chinese strategic philosophy and supports the collective obligations to the Party as the keeper of the culture and order.[114]

While an American view of transparent, integrated political interaction with all nations may imply a view towards a gradual evolution toward a more globalized world that shares Western values of liberty, free trade and freedom of access to the "shared spaces"[115] of ocean, air and space, the Chinese hold fast to their unique civilization as superior and returning as the nation at the center of the universe "by 2020"[116]. China will remain fixed and not adapt into a new form as some believe is the inevitable future of China, but continue to bring other nations under their leadership as "little brothers" within the hierarchy of a restored Sino-centric rule. A twelfth century neo-Confucian named

---

111 Chinese writings have corroborated this thought through CCP commitment of PLA forces to overseas operations that contribute to the "harmonious world" and that support what China sees as conducive to its economic growth and rising power. See. Yang Jechi's "Safeguard World Peae: Promote Common Development

112 Xi, Jinping. The Governance of China. 2015. P. 222

113 Ibid. p. 179

114 Nisbett, Richard. The Geography of Thought: How Asians and Westerners Think Differently and Why. Free Press. New York. 2003.P.16

115 The 2015 National Security Strategy re-labels global commons, a term defining international air, sea and space, into "shared spaces".

116 Xi, Jinping. The Governance of China. P.196

Lu Jiuyuan described this mentality by highlighting the connectivity between the past, the present and the future of Chinese strategic thought and the identity as a unified land within the restoration of a perpetual Sino-centric world order: "The universe is my mind and my mind is the universe. Sages appeared tens of thousands of generations ago. They shared this mind; they shared this principle. Sages will appear tens of thousands of generations to come. They will share this mind; they will share this principle."[117]

Chinese President Xi Jinping puts this thought forward in the following manner:

> For Chinese people at home and abroad, a united Chinese nation is our shared root, the profound Chinese culture is our shared soul, and the rejuvenation of the Chinese nation our shared dream. The shared root fosters eternal brotherhood, the shared soul links our hearts, and the shared dream holds us together—we will go on to write a new chapter in the history of the Chinese nation.[118]

How does this extend to space?

While the current international space legal regimes such as the OST have been ratified by the CCP, the Chinese may be heading toward a different view of where sovereignty ends. To the CCP, there is no legal demarcation that would prevent the CCP from extending sovereignty into space.[119] While the OST states in Article II that space "is not subject to national appropriation by claim of sovereignty, by means of use or occupation, or by any other means,"[120] from a legal perspective, there are troublesome indications that an increasing number of publications by influential Chinese authors advancing the principle that China's sovereign territorial airspace

---

117 Nisbett, Richard. The Geography of Thought: How Asians and Westerners Think Differently and Why. Free Press. New York. 2003 p. 17

118 Xi, Jinping. "The Rejuvenation of the Chinese Nation, a Dream Shared by All Chinese." The Governance of China. 2014. P. 69

119 Nayebi, Nima. "The Geosynchronous Orbit and the Limits of Westphalian Sovereignty." Hastings Science and Technology Law Journal. Vol 3:2, May 2010. P. 491

120 United Nations Treaty on Principles Governing the Activities of States in the Exploration and Use of Outer Space, Including the Moon and Other Celestial Bodies. 1967

extends through outer space. [121] As justification for its position, Chinese authors assert that territorial claims to outer space are not inconsistent with international law because there is no legally accepted definition of "outer space" that defines the demarcation point at which territorial airspace ends and outer space begins.[122] They then state that due to this lack of a formal agreed definition into a claim, China asserts sovereignty over all of orbital space above its territory.[123] Given the recent Chinese actions to exert sovereignty over ever expanding terrestrial land and ocean claims in the Pacific region such as the South China Sea and the East China Sea through the establishment of Economic Exclusion Zones and Air Defense Identification Zones, there are some concerns that the buildup of Chinese counterspace capabilities and the very different strategic worldview and culture of the Chinese government could lead to legal assertions by the Chinese government that the Exclusive Economic Zone and Continental Shelf Act provide legal basis for any attacks on foreign spacecraft overflying Chinese territory.[124] As Major General Cai Fengzhen and his co-authors make clear,

> The area above ground, airspace, and outer space are inseparable and integrated. They are the strategic commanding height of modern... warfare...The airspace over territorial waters and territorial lands are

---

121 United Nations Treaty on Principles Governing the Activities of States in the Exploration and Use of Outer Space, Including the Moon and Other Celestial Bodies. 1967

122 In the early days of the Space Age, there was differing interpretations on where space began and airspace ended. Since the Eisenhower Administration, while the United States does not explicitly define the demarcation between air and space, unofficial views offer 50 miles as the demarcation point when awarding astronaut status. The Soviet Union originally had a view similar to China's prior to Sputnik, however after attempts at justifying overflight of other nations, the freedom of overflight norm became customary.

123 Meek, Philip. "Testimony before the U.S.–China Economic and Security Review Commission Hearing: China's View of Sovereignty and Methods of Access Control." February 27, 2008 P.4. It is worthwhile to note the actions of the Kingdom of Tonga to claim key slots in the geostationary orbital belt, prime space real estate for space-based communications. See Edmund L. Andrews, "Tiny Tonga Seeks Satellite Empire in Space," The New York Times, August 28, 1990, found at http://www.nytimes.com/1990/08/28/business/tiny-tonga-seeks-satellite-empire-in-space.html?pagewanted=all, accessed October 12, 2015.

124 Ibid. p. 7

protected, but there is no clear standard in international law as to the altitude to which territorial airspace extends."[125]

According to Chinese government writings, in order to defend their territorial integrity on Earth and deter the perceived threats from United States or allies, these threats to Chinese interests declared in the CCP assertions of sovereignty over disputed claims in the Pacific such as Taiwan or the South China Sea island chains, gives impetus for the requirement to maintain robust and multi-layered "space attack" forces. [126] These forces must consist of "real capabilities" in order to have "effective [offensive] deterrence."

Unlike the DoD's space deterrence framework which relies upon Western values-based international agreements and codes of conduct for sustainability of the sanctuary of space, the Chinese view of space deterrence consists pri-marily of warfighting capabilities that "threaten" adversaries from using their own space and/or terrestrial capabilities against the Chinese forces pursuing their strategic objectives. [127]

In addition, Chinese negotiators in business and government are trained in the 35 Stratagems and Sun Tzu's *Art of War*. As such their negotiating style is rooted in the duality of the Confucian/Taoist teaching of cooperation cou-pled with competitive stratagems.[128] When counterpart negotiators are seen as adversaries and their interests are perceived to be in conflict, such as imposi-tions of Western values and norms that negatively impact sovereignty control and territorial integrity, the "mobile warfare" style is used. This style's pri-mary objectives are to "exhaust, destabilize, and weaken the adversary by vari-ous means, including concealment, deception, and espionage."[129]. A mobile

125 Cai and Tian. Kongtian Zhanchang yu Zhongguo Kongjun. 2006. P. 58

126 Note: Generally speaking, publications by individual researchers at AMS (Academy of Military Science) will be more authoritative than publications by researchers from other organizations like the Chinese National Defense University. Those written within the PLA proper like AMS are considered by many China scholars to be for internal use and are more reflective of the operational view of the PLA than those for open distribution.

127 Pollpeter, Kevin. China Dream, Space Dream: A Report Prepared for the U.S.-China Economic and Security Commission. IGCC. 2014.p. 12

128 Benoliel, M. "Negotiating Successfully in Asia". Eurasian Journal of Social Sciences. 1(1), 1-18. Singapore Management University. 2013. P. 7

129 Sun Zhaoli. Science of Strategy. Academy of Military Science Military Strategy Studies Dept. Beijing: Military Science Press, December 2013

warfare negotiator in space codes and treaties "will not hesitate to disseminate false information and misrepresent facts in order to mislead. Chinese negotiators often increase their bargaining edge by stimulating open competition between competitors" with the goal to "weaken the adversary."[130] Some of the stratagems used against adversaries in treaty or code of conduct negotiations include:

- **Hide a Knife behind a smile**: "Charm and ingratiate yourself to your adversaries. Once you have gained their trust, move secretly and attack them"[131]
- **Lure the tiger to leave the mountain**: Chinese throughout history have preferred to maintain "home court advantage" in negotiations and operations. This is "both psychological and physical. Whereas [Chinese] are in their natural environment, not pressed by artificial deadlines" and the cost of forward force projection, Western forces and negotiators are far from home, "cut off from headquarters, their families, and under deadline pressures"[132]
- **Await leisurely the exhausted enemy**: Chinese negotiators understand and value resources. Their goal is to preserve their own capabilities and resources, "they wage war of attrition to frustrate and deplete the counterpart psychologically and physically."[133]

This highlights how understanding strategic culture negatively impacts the NSSS "deterrent [deterrence?] through norms" that rely on the development of "norms of responsible behavior" as defined by US and European worldviews. In order to be successful in any interaction with the Chinese mode of negotiation and operations is that understanding their worldview and strategic culture is "not enough. Equally important is [having] strategic advantage."[134]

Despite this view of international negotiation and the requirement to maintain strategic advantage with capabilities such as weapons systems to threaten

---

130 Benoliel, M. "Negotiating Successfully in Asia". Eurasian Journal of Social Sciences. 1(1), 1-18. Singapore Management University. 2013. p. 7
131 Ibid. p. 15
132 Ibid. p. 15
133 Ibid. p. 15
134 Ibid. p. 16

adversaries from using their space or terrestrial capabilities, the Chinese cloak their efforts in the traditional dualistic framework of self-defense or "active defense". As one Chinese military document highlights:

> China is a Socialist state; it pursues a defensive national defense policy and a military strategy of active defense, advocates peaceful use of outer space…[and wants to] provide support and safeguarding support for socioeconomic and military activity….does not seek space hegemony [but will]…exercise the homeland's lawful space rights and ensure space security; and only when another state conscientiously infringes upon China's space rights and interests and causes harm to national space security, may China implement space deterrence against the enemy, and launch a space counterattack.[135]

In the People's Liberation Army writings on space warfare and deterrence, developing these "real capabilities" for space counterattack are considered an "integral part of battle planning by the People's Liberation Army in any future conflict."[136] This includes "periods of tension" as well as other levels of conflict. Space forces, unlike nuclear forces, are considered by Chinese military writers to be at a much lower threshold of use and therefore "space strategic power must not only have a deterrent effect, but real warfighting potential."[137]

In the Chinese language, the definition of deterrence is different than that of the Western world. While the United States views deterrence as the prevention of war through cost/benefit calculation and attempts at controlling misperception in the minds of an adversary, the Chinese word for deterrence *weishe* is a combination of coercive "punishment" strikes and deterrence.[138] This is reflected in PLA authors encouraging commanders to "gain space dominance" as "space warfare directly serves one geographical part of an entire

---

135  Sun Zhaoli. <u>Science of Strategy</u>. Academy of Military Science Military Strategy Studies Dept. Beijing: Military Science Press, December 2013.p. 238

136  Ibid.p.238

137  Ibid p.239

138  Cheng, Dean. "Chinese View of Deterrence". <u>Joint Forces Quarterly</u> Fourth Quarter, 2011.P.92

area of a war and its success or failure has immediate impact on the course and result of the war."[139]

The PLA's strategic guidance regarding deterrence requires that the PLA "must take the Party's strategic thought regarding military deterrence as [the main view] of the world, the nation and the military..."[140] The CCP and the PLA's view of the world believes that "the danger of a large-scale invasion initiated from the outside is basically ruled out...[however]..the danger of a local war triggered by the escalation of a crisis and conflicts always present, and has become an important factor interfering with...strategic opportunities for national development."[141]

The focus of all deterrence operations, including in the space domain for the PLA, is to effectively deter behaviors that endanger China's core interests and major interests through enhancing military capabilities to fight for the initiative of the strategic overall situation.[142] In order to create the means to achieve the initiative in the overall strategic situation requires "powerful comprehensive national power" to provide for effective deterrence effects. This valid or credible threat is only possible when looked at from, as Chinese military writings put it, as "integrated-whole" deterrence. Once this is achieved, then demonstrating the political will combined with the capability to achieve victory then and only then, would the PLA and the CCP be ready to "conduct the activity in a concerted way, and successfully perform full preparations for going from deterrence to war to impose powerful strategic pressure on the opponent."[143]

How does the PLA organize their concept for space deterrence? First, according to PLA writings, the integration of space with other military forces is important in order to form the most effective military force possible. By having the strongest military force possible, says Chinese authors, can a

---

139 Pollpeter, Kevin. <u>China Dream, Space Dream: A Report Prepared for the U.S.-China Economic and Security Commission</u>. IGCC. 2014.p. iv

140 Sun Zhaoli. <u>Science of Strategy</u>. Academy of Military Science Military Strategy Studies Dept. Beijing: Military Science Press, December 2013.p. 190

141 Ibid. p. 190

142 Sun Zhaoli. <u>Science of Strategy</u>. Academy of Military Science Military Strategy Studies Dept. Beijing: Military Science Press, December 2013.p. 191

143 Sun Zhaoli. <u>Science of Strategy</u>. Academy of Military Science Military Strategy Studies Dept. Beijing: Military Science Press, December 2013.p. 194

nation deter other nations from attacking it.[144] This view has been seen in recent orders by President Xi Jinping for space to become integrated in all aspects of Chinese military operations.[145] Second is having a credible counterspace capability to threaten other nation's space assets in order to deter the opponent from using its counterspace capabilities. "In this way, both sides would be reluctant to attack the others space assets lest they also come under attack."[146]

In addition to having a credible counterspace capability for effective space deterrence, the Chinese advocate that they should reveal "firm resolve to dare to and prepare to use this capability" in order to create "certain psychological pressure on and fear in the adversary, and [force] the adversary to dare not conduct space operations with initiative."[147] This includes conducting "limited space operational activities with warning and punishment as goals" as a means of de-escalation of the crisis.[148] This view of force-dependent deterrence reads more like a traditional deterrent model than even the present DoD space deterrence framework that purposely avoids a credible threat of counteraction in the event of an attack on U.S. space assets. As PLA writers state, the goal of deterrence is to "choose appropriate deterrence means to display the horribleness, severity, and urgency of the consequences."[149]

If a "period of tension" arises, Chinese writers state that it is vital to achieving strategic objectives terrestrially to "deliver destructive strikes to the enemy using maximum power in order to fight rapidly, conclude the operation rapidly and to withdraw from the confrontation."[150]

---

144 Pollpeter, Kevin. China Dream, Space Dream: A Report Prepared for the U.S.-China Economic and Security Commission. IGCC. 2014.p. iv

145 "China Military Aims to Build Up Space Defences" Sky News Online. 15 Apr 2014. http://news.sky.com/story/1242772/china-military-aims-to-build-up-space-defences

146 Pollpeter, Kevin. "The Chinese Vision of Space Military Operations". The Paradox of Power. NDU Press. 2011. P. 342

147 Sun Zhaoli. Science of Strategy. Academy of Military Science Military Strategy Studies Dept. Beijing: Military Science Press, December 2013.p. 234

148 Ibid. p. 234

149 Sun Zhaoli. Science of Strategy. Academy of Military Science Military Strategy Studies Dept. Beijing: Military Science Press, December 2013.p. 192

150 Pollpeter, Kevin. China Dream, Space Dream: A Report Prepared for the U.S.-China Economic and Security Commission. IGCC. 2014.p. 106

As seen in the Chinese strategic culture that views the world and the international system in a holistic manner, the same holds true with their view of the many "zones" that the space domain covers with respect to space deterrence.

"[It] covers vast areas (zones) from the cosmos at tens of thousands of kilometers from the Earth to the Earth's surface, with many areas [zones] forming an organic whole...space military struggle...[is] a synthesis of many types of correlated military activity, including space to space, space to ground, and ground to ground."[151]

The Chinese do not "share the same interests" in the space domain or a view of enhancing the status quo of a U.S.-dominated international order. They are, according to many scholars, on a "quest for wealth and power."[152] As one author stated, the Chinese are "no longer guided by Maoist proletariat ideology, [and] now see [space]...technology as a major factor in its rise as a world power as it seeks increased influence and independence. China's pursuit of spacepower is a reflection of this emphasis on technology and its grand strategy to "regain the nation's former status as a great power that controls its own fate."[153]

Despite the NSSS' goal of preventing the development, testing, and deployment of space weapons systems, the Chinese possess the most rapidly maturing space program in the world and are using on-orbit and ground based assets to support China's national economic, military and political goals and objectives.[154] China has, according to a recent Pentagon report, "invested in advanced space capabilities, with particular emphasis on satellite communications, intelligence surveillance and reconnaissance (ISR), satellite navigation, and meteorology, as well as...a vast ground infrastructure supporting spacecraft and space launch vehicle manufacture, command and control, and data

---

151 Sun Zhaoli. op. cit., p., 231.

152 Pollpeter, Kevin. China Dream, Space Dream: A Report Prepared for the U.S.-China Economic and Security Commission. IGCC. 2014.p. 106

153 Ibid.p. 106

154 2015 Annual Report to Congress: Military and Security Developments Involving the People's Republic of China. P. 13

downlink."[155] In addition to this supporting infrastructure, the PLA "continues to develop a variety of capabilities designed to...prevent the use of space... by adversaries during a crisis or conflict including the development of directed-energy weapons and satellite jammers."[156]

In addition, since the ASAT test in January 2007, the Chinese have continued to develop and test ground launched kinetic interceptors for space attack, with testing since 2007 being non-destructive. The 2015 *DoD Report to Congress on Chinese Military Developments* discusses several tests of Low Earth Orbit (LEO) capable interceptors as well as tests that appear to highlight a Geostationary Earth Orbit (GEO) capable interceptor capable of reaching at least 22,300 miles. These test programs indicate that while the DoD space deterrence framework speaks to the DoD's stated deterrence and dissuasion of testing of counterspace weapons systems, China has not given any indication of ceasing these tests or of PLA development of doctrine for space warfighting because of the four element approach of DoD space deterrence. Why would this be? According to Chinese military authors, testing and development of space and counterspace technology is important for effective space deterrence:

> "Even in a relatively peaceful period, under circumstances where a hostile relationship is unclear, the presence and development of one side's space systems and the boosting of its space capability, still can potentially influence and constrain the military activity of other nations and generate a certain deterrent effect."[157]

As mentioned earlier, some DoD analysts believe that transparency of military space activities is vital for preventing the use of outer space for military engagements of either reversible or destructive means. However, given the very different worldview and strategic culture of Chinese decision makers to the space domain and their historical and long term view of the international

---

155  Ibid. p. 14

156  Ibid. p. 14

157  Sun Zhaoli. <u>Science of Strategy</u>. Academy of Military Science Military Strategy Studies Dept. Beijing: Military Science Press, December 2013.p. 234

order, this foundational view of the DoD Space Deterrence framework has not improved the security of American assets in space.

The Western mindset sees "transparency and openness as the surest way to peace" and believes that "when one state can effectively monitor another, fears of surprise attack are mitigated, and the tendency to overestimate a potential opponent's capacities and intentions are minimized. With transparency, the security dilemma is obviated and cooperation is possible."[158] However, this is not the way the Chinese see transparency and openness. As one author correctly describes:

> To a [Chinese] strategist, letting an opponent know precisely one's strengths and weaknesses merely invites attack. The key to stability in this view is uncertainty--not knowing how strong or how weak an opponent is and never, under any circumstances, revealing one's own strengths or weaknesses. The more sure the knowledge, the more crafty the countervailing plan, the more likely its success.[159]

Why should we shun transparency, embrace adaptability and unpredictability in our spacepower strategic support planning? Xi Jinping sums this view up when he stated that:

> Boasting a vast land of 9.6 million sq km, a rich cultural heritage and a strong bond among the 1.3 billion Chinese people, we are resolved to go our own way.... We must not blindly copy the...models of other countries nor accept their dictation...As a Chinese saying goes, "Standing firm when assailed by rain and wind from all directions, our confidence is supported by our core values"[160]

Given the long history of "humiliation" and weakness at the hands of Western "unequal treaties" and the establishment of the current UN system (created without the Chinese Communist Party's involvement) transparency is not

---

158 Dolman, Everett. "New Frontiers, Old Realities." <u>Strategic Studies Quarterly</u>. Spring 2012. P. 83

159 Ibid. p. 83

160 Xi, Jinping. <u>The Governance of China</u>. Foreign Language Press. Beijing. 2015. P. 191

something that can be assumed with the Chinese government. It goes against the Chinese strategic culture of secrecy and deception in negotiation style as mentioned earlier and would create an impression of weakness domestically and internationally of the CCP. Due to this the CCP may view the sharing of such information as detrimental to their survival as the keepers of the strategic culture, governance and the PLA's power and not a mutually beneficial path toward preservation of a Western dominated status quo. If capabilities are shared with the potential "enemy" it would be to "selectively...reveal China's space technology and space capability, and adopt an oppositional mode to reduce their expectations for space weaponization and to increase their degree of difficulty and costs in space weaponization."[161]

During peacetime however, PLA strategic guidance on deterrence recommends a combination of hiding one's capabilities and keeping a low profile with active actions for war preparations such as testing and escalation control to include low-intensity warfare "until our deterrence goal is realized."[162] This highlights the value of avoiding transparency as part of a long term stratagem ignoring the ineffective American course of action of transparency as part of the NSSS deterrence concept.

Instead, the United States should utilize uncertainty like the Chinese, given uncertainty enables friction that can create foundational strategic impediments for the adversary. The current strategic situation in space and on Earth, due to American and allied inaction, enables the Chinese to gather information and offensive capabilities needed to shape the strategic environment to the PLA advantage while giving the U.S. leadership the perception that the United States is winning when in fact they are losing to complex Chinese deterrence activities imposing friction on US and allied space operations and terrestrial strategy.[163] Clausewitz describes this phenomenon well when he stated:

Friction (which includes the intersection of many factors, such as uncertainty, psychological/moral forces and effects, etc.) impedes

---

161  Sun Zhaoli. op. cit..p. 240

162  Ibid.p. 195

163  Benoliel, M. "Negotiating Successfully in Asia". Eurasian Journal of Social Sciences. 1(1), 1-18. Singapore Management University. 2013. p. 15

activity. Friction is the only concept that more or less corresponds to the factors that distinguish real war from war on paper.[164]

A more recent strategic theorist, Colonel John Boyd, USAF, stated:

Operate inside adversary's observation-orientation-decision-action loops to enmesh adversary in a world of uncertainty, doubt, mistrust, confusion, disorder, fear, panic chaos ...and/or fold adversary back inside himself so that he cannot cope with events/efforts as they unfold.[165]

Why would these two strategic thinkers focus on friction and uncertainty? Because the atmosphere of war is friction, friction is generated and magnified by menace, ambiguity, deception, rapidity, uncertainty, mistrust, etc. These are the actions that the Chinese are engaged in space and in their increasingly belligerent and expansionist activities in the Asia Pacific region. This friction in the strategic sense, is the opposite and de-stabilizing side of the strategic Tao, with harmony/initiative generated by "rapidity and variety" leading to strategic success for China using the Observation, Orient, Decision, Action loop or also known as the Decision Calculus Loop.[166] As Sun Tzu was cited as saying, "Those who use arms well, cultivate the Way (Tao)..."[167]

Orientation, seen as a result, represents what Boyd referred to as "images, views or impressions of the world shaped by genetic heritage, cultural tradition, previous experiences, and unfolding circumstances."[168] In other words, Boyd is defining what is called strategic culture today and is defined by Kartchner as "that set of shared beliefs, assumptions, and modes of behavior, derived from common experiences and accepted narratives (both oral and written), that shape collective identity and relationships to other groups, and which determine appropriate ends and means for achieving security objectives."[169]

---

164 Quoted from Boyd brief on Organic Design of C2 1990

165 Quoted from Boyd brief on Organic Design of C2 1990

166 Boyd, John. "Organic Design of Command and Control". Presentation. 1990.

167 Sun Tzu. The Art of War. Shambhala Dragon Edition. Boston. 1988.p. 91

168 Boyd, John op. cit.

169 Kartchner, Kerry et al. Strategic Culture and Weapons of Mass Destruction: Culturally based Insights into Comparative National Security Policymaking. Palgrave-Macmillan. 2009. P.9

Once the DoD strategists and policymakers grasp these important aspects of strategic context, understanding that the Chinese are doing the same thing as part of their analysis, they can take that information and orient the nation's strategic posture based on the patterns discerned relating to adversary activities and at the same time denying our adversary the possibility of discerning patterns that match our activity as part of our strategy execution.[170]

A few examples of Chinese strategic patterns of behavior include their use of force within crisis situations over time. For example, surprise is a very important pattern of force projection within the PLA. In October 1962, China conducted operations against India due to territorial disputes. The Chinese launched major, rapid attacks, which succeeded immediately. After a short pause, "the Chinese renewed their attacks in mid-November" using the doctrines of the classic Chinese strategist, Sun Tzu. These include: "all warfare is based on deception….therefore, when capable, feign incapacity; when active, inactivity….Pretend inferiority and encourage [adversary] arrogance…Attack where he is unprepared; sally out when he does not expect you….These are the strategist's key to victory. It is not possible to discuss them beforehand."[171] Thus in order to be victorious, it is not beneficial to achieve strategic success through TCBMs; rather surprise attacks and deception are key to strategic victory.

Secondly, another pattern is achievement of psychological and political shock. While some commentators such as Michael Krepon may believe that Chinese offensive deterrence strikes are "unlikely," this highlights the lack of real observational understanding of the strategic culture and doctrines of the PLA.[172] Psychological or political shock of a pre-emptive strike may be the payoff that the PLA is looking for rather than simply trying to gain a complete military advantage over U.S. capabilities. As a result, a rapid, destructive, limited attack with kinetic energy anti-satellites (KE ASATs) could create conditions that lead the United States or its allies to "become disheartened and defeatist as a result of the unexpected reverse he has suffered and may be induced to reduce his war aims" or perhaps change U.S. policy objectives in

---

170 Boyd, John. "op. cit.

171 Burles, Mark. Patterns in China's Use of Force: Evidence from History and Doctrinal Writings.RAND. p. 8

172 Krepon, Michael. "Space and Nuclear Deterrence". Anti-Satellite Weapons, Deterrence and Sino-American Relations. Stimson Center. 2013. P. 31

the Pacific to the Chinese advantage.[173] What is more, is that achieving such a psychological-political shock is magnified in the case of a military force that has limited force-projection and sustainment capabilities, such as the current posture of the DoD space forces that only contains reversible means of counterspace operations.

An example of psychological shock leading to policy changes for an adversary is again found in the 1962 India campaign where the PLA adopted a punishment strategy that undercut Indian self-confidence[174]. By doing so, "the Chinese achieved a more rapid and decisive change in policy than would likely have emerged from a long-drawn-out negotiation in which the Chinese tried to trade the captured territory for an Indian recognition of Chinese ownership of the territories they held before the border war began."[175] Some may argue that a Chinese attack on U.S. or allied space systems is unlikely because the [military] benefits would not outweigh the costs. However, a counterargument can be made that DoD strategists and policymakers lack sufficient understanding of the strategic culture needed to properly orient the American space posture to be prepared to decide and act when necessary to protect space systems.

In addition, it is important to note that China has even used force not only to settle a crisis such as that with India, but also have "typically used force to create a crisis."[176] Understanding this unique strategic orientation of the PLA forces is vital to understand the strategic reality as it is, and not as some would like it to be, to ensure American strategic interests and homeland are properly secured in space and terrestrially.

The view of having space weapons as a means of CCP survival and territorial integrity through robust military power is key to understanding the linkage that Chinese military writers have of spacepower with nuclear weapons as well. The Chinese view the nexus of spacepower and nuclear weapons not as separate domains of operations, but rather as "an

---

173 Ibid. p. 10
174 Burles, Mark. Patterns in China's Use of Force: Evidence from History and Doctrinal Writings. RAND.2000.p. 13
175 Ibid p. 12
176 Ibid. p. 16

integrated-whole composite strength for strategic deterrence."[177] As one PLA author stated:

> The party that enjoys superiority in space will secure its survival by weakening the enemy's nuclear deterrent capabilities, thereby increasing tremendously one's nuclear deterrent power. Space forces constitute both a space shield and a space sword.[178]

This quote highlights another disturbing yet important reality for American strategic planners to grasp: the development of space attack systems and a credible deterrent threat against U.S. systems also include the attacking of nuclear command and control space support segments. As the same PLA author describes this in further detail:

> "Commanders should actively take the initiative to strike at an enemy's vital targets because "only through active offensive operations and counter-attacks can one seize and maintain the initiative. Specifically, vital targets include information, command and support systems. Hitting these vital targets through concentrated strikes is especially recommended in cases where the PLA faces a "powerful enemy equipped with high technology weapons and equipment" rather than conduct wars of annihilation…the first targets of a campaign…are the detection, command and telecommunications information systems, whose degradation or destruction will negate or reduce the enemy's ability to control information and create conditions for later combat."[179]

Chinese military strategists recommend attacking these key information and command and control nodes because PLA analysts assess that space-based information

---

177 Sun Zhaoli. <u>Science of Strategy</u>. Academy of Military Science Military Strategy Studies Dept. Beijing: Military Science Press, December 2013.p. 239
178 Ibid. p. 155
179 Ibid. p. 156

"...will become a deciding factor in future wars, that space will be the dominant battlefield, and that in order to achieve victory on Earth and preserve sovereignty control of Chinese territory and expanding core interests, the PLA must first seize the initiative in space. This will require China to achieve space supremacy, defined as the ability to freely use space and to deny the use of space to adversaries."[180]

Moreover, "the assessment that *space is the dominant battlefield* [emphasis added] has led PLA analysts to conclude that war in space is inevitable."[181]

Chinese leaders and strategists have increasingly regarded the dominance of space as critical to their domestic and international security transformation- which the CCP considers intertwined.[182] Hu Jintao noted in 2004 that the "progress of the times" and Chinese economic development were pushing Chinese security interests into space and that the space domain along with the maritime regions were the two critical areas of Chinese expansion.[183] Furthermore, he stated:

"With the opening up and development of our country's economy, our national interests have gradually gone beyond the scope of traditional land territory, territorial waters, and territorial airspace. In order to safeguard our ever-expanding national interests, military strategy needs to expand its vision, not only paying attention to and safeguarding our country's interests in survival, but also paying attention to and safeguarding our country's developmental interests; not only paying attention to and safeguarding traditional security of land territory, [we must pay] attention to...

---

180 Pollpeter, Kevin. China Dream, Space Dream: China's Progress in Space Technologies and Implications for the United States. IGCC.2015. p. 107

181 Pollpeter, Kevin. China Dream, Space Dream: China's Progress in Space Technologies and Implications for the United States. IGCC.2015. p. 107

182 Chinese President Xi Jinping stated in his April 24, 2014 speech to the Central Policy Commission, " All regions and government agencies should implement China's holistic view of national security, and acquire an understanding of the new characteristics and trends...We should attach equal importance to external and internal security ...our own security and the common security of the world." P. 224

183 Tanner, Scott. China's Emerging National Security Interests and their Impact on the People's Liberation Army. Marine Corps University. 2015.p.65

safeguarding security in such areas as the ocean, space and information. In order to provide strategic support for the expansion of national interests."[184]

This statement is just one of many that highlights the expanding list of "core interests" that China expects other nations, including the United States, to respect despite not reciprocating the respect of other nations' core national interests such as Japan or the United States.[185] Understanding and observing this unique identity demonstrates the importance in the Chinese strategic calculus of the connection of harmony and friction to achieve strategic success. Strategic success within complex endeavors such as deterrence of war, or the prevention of and/or preparing for war in space, has been defined by one American strategic theorist to include dominance in utilization of time and space with effective means, but more importantly, effectively staying ahead of the adversary's "mental, moral and physical" aspects of strategy.[186] This requires understanding the adversary's (in this case-Chinese decision makers) unique decision calculus, in order to ensure one has the appropriate strategy for spacepower to support with deterrence-but a deterrence that requires strength, focus and vision to achieve strategic success.[187]

In making this assessment, Chinese writings are similar to U.S. writings on space from the 1950s and 1960s. This includes "a universal belief that space is the strategic high ground, and a prominent role for manned military space missions, including the use of manned military space planes, space stations, and lunar bases."[188] One type of "vital target" related to "informationalization" (gaining information dominance) is America's space-based ISR assets. As Kevin Pollpeter noted in his recent report, "The denial of overhead capabilities integrated with cyber and kinetic attacks against non-space based C4ISR nodes could greatly complicate the ability of the U.S. military to flow

---

184 Ibid. p. 64

185 Ibid. p. 64

186 Osinga, Frans P.B. Science, Strategy and War: The Strategic Theory of John Boyd. Rutledge Press. p.213

187 Boyd, John. "Organic Design for Command and Control". Presentation. 1990.

188 Pollpeter, Kevin. China Dream, Space Dream: A Report Prepared for the U.S.-China Economic and Security Commission. IGCC. 2014. P. 107

forces to the region and to conduct operations effectively."[189] ISR capabilities it should be noted are viewed as key because, unlike the Western view of overhead ISR satellites serving as a stabilizing function, allowing for knowledge of potential adversaries to prevent miscalculation, Chinese military strategists and CCP leaders view this capability to be "battlefield preparation" and not for stabilization.[190] Chinese analysts have stated that "battlefield situational awareness is the core of information age warfare...which means that one must be able to destroy or jam the systems that are fundamental to that situational awareness."[191]

This plan for Chinese space deterrence focuses on "rapid, destructive" engagements on the "low-threshold" types of U.S. space systems that are "easy to attack and difficult to defend" as well as "select attacks against the critical node [s] of enemy space systems" to exploit the heavy reliance on space systems for peacetime and wartime operations in the Pacific.[192]

## Chapter Conclusions

The manifestation of Chinese strategic culture in the development of negotiations of space treaties, codes of conduct, and conventions as well as PLA offensive space deterrence doctrines highlights serious gaps in the National Security Space Strategy's four elements approach to deterring potential near peer adversaries such as the Chinese. In addition to not fitting the classical definition of deterrence from a Western perspective as highlighted in Chapter 1, the NSSS space deterrence concept does not prevent the Chinese concept of "attack to deter" in space, but rather continues on a path that keeps US and allied systems vulnerable and may very well provide the easy-to-strike targets capable of doing grave damage to U.S. force projection capabilities as well as economic and societal stability within the homeland.

The Chinese have a unique view of the world and themselves, and the space domain. China's strategic culture is not the same as that of the American

---

189 Ibid. p. 108

190 Wortzel, Larry. <u>The Dragon Extends its Reach</u>. Potomac Books.2012 P. 126

191 Ibid. p. 126

192 Sun Zhaoli. <u>Science of Strategy</u>. Academy of Military Science Military Strategy Studies Dept. Beijing: Military Science Press, December 2013.p. 240

culture, and promotes a more active, offensive form of deterrence than the one found in the NSSS. This strategic culture is based on a long view of history as well as an understanding that the world is not a linear process but a complex, constantly changing place where the struggle and victory of harmony over friction is key to the China Dream of regaining their leadership position as the dominant nation. As keeper of the Tao or Way toward harmony in the world, the PLA plan for space dominance through active defense and rapid, destructive space warfare places US space systems vulnerable to surprise attack. The United States must develop means to deter Chinese counter-intervention strategies supported by their space attack infrastructures they believe will aid the achievement of terrestrial objectives in the Pacific and worldwide for the Chinese government.

# CHAPTER 3

## Creating A Tiered, Tailored, Triad: Defending The U.S. Space Infrastructure

> *Most governments when asked to choose between war and peace are likely to choose peace because it looks safer. These same governments if asked to choose between getting the first or second strike will very likely choose the first strike... once they feel war is inevitable, or even very probable...*
> HERMAN KAHN, ON THERMONUCLEAR WAR 1960

> *Space fighting is not far off. National security has already exceeded territory and territorial waters and airspace and territorial space should also be added. The modes of defense will no longer be to fight on our own territory and fight for marine rights and interests. We must also engage in space defense as well as air defense.*
> TENG JIANQUN, PEOPLE'S LIBERATION ARMY ANALYST, 2001

American space infrastructure is not only an inherent strategic asset for the United States; space supporting ground and orbital segments are also a vital piece of the nation's critical defense infrastructure.[193] As such, it is a key center of gravity for America's instruments of national power. This fact is not lost on potential adversaries such as the People's Republic of

---

193 DoDD 3020.40, "Defense Critical Infrastructure Protection Program," (2013) declares spacepower to be defense critical infrastructure.

China who have assessed that spacepower is America's "soft ribs."[194] Due to the continued integration of space capabilities and applications into American society, PLA writings highlight the "grave aftermath" that would result if U.S. space systems are destroyed or incapacitated.[195] This all points to the need for U.S. decision-makers to ensure that U.S. space capabilities are protected and available to support the safety and prosperity of the U.S. population, homeland defense and, when needed, force projection worldwide to defend national interests in the forward regions such as space itself.[196]

Unfortunately, the NSSS' concept of deterrence has not protected our critical space infrastructure from purposeful interference nor has it deterred the development, testing and deployment of offensive space attack systems. The DoD Space Policy speaks of purposeful interference when it states "purposeful interference with U.S. space systems, including their supporting infrastructure, will be considered an infringement of U.S. rights."[197] This chapter will explore what is needed to create an effective and credible space deterrence posture.

## Readiness for Chinese Rapid, Destructive Wars in Space

The PLA has stated in their recent strategy documents that future wars, including those that begin in or extend to space, are to be "destructive" in nature and rapidly executed to achieve their objectives.[198] This rapid, destructive warfare includes the development, testing and deployment of KE ASAT interceptors as part of the Chinese multi-pronged "space attack architectures".

The strategic reality that the true norm of behavior in space is that of reversible, yet purposeful interference, highlights how the DoD space deterrence construct within the National Security Space Strategy has failed. In addition, the employment of KE ASATs, a developed, tested, and deployed, survivable mobile warfare approach in China, highlights another partial failure of this

---

194 Tellis, Ashley J. "China's Military Space Strategy", Survival: Global Politics and Strategy, 49:3. 2012. P.49

195 Sun Zhaoli. Science of Strategy. Academy of Military Science Military Strategy Studies Dept. Beijing: Military Science Press, December 2013.p.

196 Joint Publication 3-27 Homeland Defense (2013) states that space operations are conducted to support homeland defense.

197 DoDD 3100.10 DoD Space Policy. October 2012. P.1

198 Johnson-Freese, Joan. Space as a Strategic Asset. Columbia Univ Press. 2007. P. 222

deterrence concept on the non-reversible side of the spectrum. Therefore, because the United States lacks a credible, effective deterrent to the use of reversible counterspace attacks upon the space sector of American critical infrastructure, the use of KE ASATs in an active, surprise attack campaign is still a threat to be deterred from use against American and allied interests.

The Chinese development of "mobile warfare" ASAT missile systems for both Low Earth Orbit (LEO) and Geosynchronous Earth Orbit (GEO) altitudes provides the PLA space forces with the ability to conduct a first strike against the critical infrastructure of the homeland and armed forces, while the U.S. does not have a dedicated program or strategy to mitigate this threat.[199] This constitutes a first-strike *instability* in the favor of Chinese space forces.[200]

First-strike stability or instability is related to a concept that Glenn Kent and David Thaler of The RAND Corporation developed in 1989 to examine the dynamics of deterrence between two or more nuclear states.[201] Forrest Morgan, also from RAND, states that this concept is similar to crisis stability, which is "a measure of the countries' incentives not to preempt in a crisis, that is, not to attack first in order to beat the attack of the enemy."[202] This thought process did not review the psychological or strategic culture factors present in the specific crisis. Rather, first-strike stability focuses on each side's force posture and "balance of capabilities and vulnerabilities that could make a crisis unstable should a confrontation occur."[203]

Space, like the nuclear realm, is an environment with substantial incentives for striking first should war appear probable, or in the case of Chinese strategic culture and doctrine, if war can be deterred through coercive military actions or demonstrations in space.[204] However, unlike the nuclear realm, space is an "offense-dominant domain, which is to say that holding space targets at risk is far easier and cheaper than defending them."[205] Thus, American

---

199  2015 <u>DoD Report on Chinese Military Power</u> 2015. P. 13-14

200  Morgan, Forrest. <u>Deterrence and First Strike Stability in Space</u>. RAND Corporation.2010.p. 2

201  Ibid. p. 2

202  Ibid. P.2

203  Ibid. p. 1-2

204  Ibid. P. 2

205  Finch, Jay. "Bringing Space Crisis Stability Down to Earth." <u>Joint Forces Quarterly 76,</u> 1<sup>st</sup> Qtr, 2015. P. 18

space-based and related ground critical infrastructure provides a major center of gravity (COG) vulnerable for an adversary to target and damage life and prosperity for American society.

Another way to see this is through an updated view of Warden's Rings[206]. As seen in Figure 1, each of the rings highlights a rung of a strategic air campaign leading to the center ring which is the senior leadership or command and control, of the infrastructure, military forces, etc. Given the interdependencies of the space infrastructure with other areas of critical homeland importance, it is possible that a well-executed "space Pearl Harbor" type operation could simultaneously create damaging effects upon all of the rings at once.

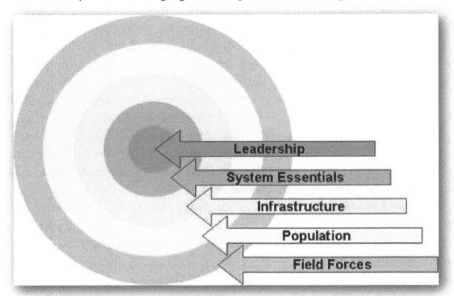

Figure 1: Warden's Five Rings of Strategic Attack

Thus, as Bruce MacDonald, a leading voice on space warfare and the author of the Council on Foreign Relations book *China, Anti-Satellites Weapons and U.S. Space Security*, in testimony to the House Strategic Forces Subcommittee correctly states:

206 Warden's Rings is a concept of strategic air campaign planning developed by Col John A. Warden III prior to the First Persian Gulf War in 1991. It was articulated in his book The Enemy as a System. See Figure 1, page 56, for the list of the rings for strategic attack on an adversary.

"The U.S. has an overriding interest in maintaining the safety, survival, and function of its space assets so that the profound military, civilian, and commercial benefits they enable can continue to be available to the United States and its allies."[207]

To maintain the survival of U.S. space assets will require the acknowledgement of a few important factors at the strategic level. First, protection and survival will require the acknowledgement that our space assets (both terrestrial and space segments) are critical infrastructure to our nation's economy and the international financial system.

Federal policies, including those within the DoD, highlight the importance of the space sector to the many other parts of defense and national critical infrastructure. Recent reports have highlighted that due to growing interdependencies between critical infrastructure areas such as communications, transportation, energy and defense, there is a "potentially a large cost in human life...or economic markets" if and when they fail.[208] Criteria that define what makes infrastructure within the United States critical include: 1) provide routine functions along operational paths essential for average or routine system function 2) no handy, rapid substitutes exist, 3) sudden dysfunction in and around these elements causes nontrivial harm, and 4) they are embedded in wide, functionally reciprocal, integrated systems."[209] The more critical that these interdependencies become, the "larger the cost of failure [they] are likely to have."[210] One small part of the larger space sector that is interdependent with the transportation, defense, energy and other infrastructure sectors is reliance upon the Global Positioning System (GPS) navigation and timing signal. As one report states, "Because of the increasing reliance of transportation upon GPS, the consequences of loss of the GPS signal can be severe (depending upon its application), in terms of safety and...economic

---

207 Bruce W. MacDonald, Testimony before the Strategic Forces Subcommittee, House Armed Forces Committee, March 18, 2009

208 Egan, Matthew Jude. "Anticipating Future Vulnerability: Defining Characteristics of Increasingly Critical Infrastructure-like Systems." Journal of Contingencies and Crisis Management. Vol 15, No 1. March 2007

209 Egan, Matthew Jude. "Anticipating Future Vulnerability: Defining Characteristics of Increasingly Critical Infrastructure-like Systems." Journal of Contingencies and Crisis Management. Vol 15, No 1. March 2007. P. 8

210 Ibid. p. 9

damage to the nation."[211] Another vulnerability related to GPS is the reliance of the energy infrastructure on the GPS timing signal. One report summarizes this concern as follows:

"GPS has emerged as a key component of the power generation and distribution network monitoring systems for data collection, fault detection, vulnerability mitigation, and recovery. With its continued market penetration, the value of GPS to the power industry is likely to grow, along with the impacts of unanticipated disruptions."[212]

Second, strategic reality in space requires an acknowledgement that active defense, in concert with passive defense measures, of US space infrastructures are vital to maintain information dominance in both diplomatic and military instruments of national power as well as support to include homeland defense and overseas force projection in defense of US interests as well as allied defense treaty obligations. For example, James G. Lee of Air University wrote:

"…since information dominance can create uncertainty regarding the focus and thrust of the theater campaign, offensive counterspace operations should normally precede other theater operations. To attain information dominance, offensive counterspace operations should use a combination of [kinetic and non-kinetic] weapon systems to attack the operational center of gravity of a space system. Depending on the space system, the enemy, and the level of conflict, the center of gravity can be located in any of the three segments of an enemy's space system."[213]

The Chinese understand this as part of the counter-intervention strategy with their space attack system enabled "informationalization." As such, in order for

---

211 U.S. Department of Transportation. Vulnerability of the Transportation System Reliance on the Global Positioning System. Report from the National Transportation Systems Center. August, 2001. P. ES-6

212 U.S. Department of Transportation. Global Positioning System Timing Signal Criticality Update. Report from the National Transportation Systems Center. July 2008. P. xii

213 Lee, James G., Counterspace Operations for Information Dominance. Air University Press. 1995, P. 126

the United States to generate sufficient friction and uncertainty in the mind of an adversary, information dominance supplied through counterspace operations is a must. This can be accomplished through "soft kill" or a "hard kill" and depending on what type of space power the US employs, could target ground segment or space segment. [214]

Fourth, strategists must acknowledge that space is an offense dominant domain and in order to provide effective deterrence, the United States must actively protect its space systems through a credible offensive counterforce capability to reverse the first-strike instability due to the Chinese KE ASATs and their satellite reconstitution launch capacity.

While some assert that first strike stability is something that can be gained through the present NSSS, the facts as observed show the opposite is true. Space is indeed unique from other domains, but not in the way that some describe it. Space is an offensive dominant domain and as such, defense is challenging especially in the kinetic, irreversible sphere. As a result, the Chinese view of deterrence makes much more sense in assuring space protection than the NSSS' view of space deterrence. In this view, the posturing of forces for use as kinetic strikes against critical space infrastructure can be viewed as an escalation of threat and therefore, this threat to the homeland and interests of the nation should be neutralized before the attack can be made against whatever target or system is at risk. Mao once said he believed the Western view of waiting until one was attacked to be too passive.[215] Our current posture attempts to treat space as if there is a means to defense, while not providing for a defense or real protection of this vital resource for our homeland.

Finally, American strategists should recognize that deterrence requires getting into an adversary's decision process through observation and analysis of their strategic culture, doctrine, and strategic behavior; orient the U.S. force posture accordingly and be prepared to engage in military operations preventatively when necessary to actively defend space infrastructure and maintain escalation dominance in crisis or conflict.

Deterrence, or war prevention, requires an understanding of the adversary, the adversary leadership's decision cycle informed by its strategic culture and resulting worldview. Deterrence must be focused on the adversary senior

---

214 Ibid. p. 127-128
215 Kissinger, Henry. <u>On China</u>. Penguin Press. 2011. P. 133

leadership's decision processes and not the individual citizen of China, the adversary leaders' means of commanding and controlling forces and shaping the strategic and operational levels through the holding of vital adversary targets at risk. How does one accomplish this strategic deterrence formulation between a Western nation that traditionally relies on its near term technological gains, training, and linear based tactical planning to formulate operational objectives and strategic end states against a potential adversary that thinks holistically, identifies themselves collectively and maintains a long term vision?

The U.S. senior leadership must develop a realistic strategy that DoD/IC spacepower can support and that highlights the unique space domain defense requirements in order to effectively protect its space based critical infrastructure. How can the United States gain real, effective deterrence in the Pacific? Understanding the adversary decision calculus is the first step. This requires observation into the adversary command and control structures and processes.

The United States defense leadership should create a space support strategy that enables the means to remove the perception that attacking space infrastructure is a low-threshold action that will have no response in kind. This perception has led the PLA down the path of creating space weapons as part of the Chinese overarching counter-intervention strategy which targets the vulnerability of the architecture, the perceived lack of will to actively defend those assets or counter those increasing risks to American way of life and operations. In short, the US must remove the temptation to strike at what has become the image of "soft ribs" for both deterrence of attack on the homeland as well as extended deterrence protections of allies as well. This image must be reversed. How? We must act upon the knowledge and understanding of strategic reality and use our resources at a faster tempo or rhythm than our adversaries.

One way to do this is to take what America already has in current programs of record, across multiple services and agencies and flip the Tao on its head. The United States should exploit operations and weapons that:

- Generate a rapidly changing environment (quick/clear observations, orientation and decisions, fast-tempo, fast transient maneuvers, leading to quick kill when needed)
- Inhibit a potential adversary's capacity to adapt to such an environment by clouding or distorting their observations, orientation and decision calculus

- Simultaneously improve our own command and control and space force posture, offensive deterrence capabilities and options for senior leaders to compress our own time to decision and actions (kinetic or non-kinetic), while stretching out the adversary's time to generate a favorable mismatch in time/ability to shape and adapt to change.
- The goal would be to collapse the Chinese's current strategy of counter-intervention (supported and enabled by multi-layered space forces) into confusion and disorder by causing them to over or under react to activity that appears simultaneously menacing as well as ambiguous, chaotic, or misleading. In short, the goal is to get ahead in their own strategic game of expansion and domination of the space environment as well as the terrestrial engagements supported by offensive space deterrence.[216]

## Counter-Strategy Part 1: Integrate Space into Homeland Defense Strategy

As PLA space systems are tied to the homeland defense of the Chinese mainland, space systems are also a part of American critical defense infrastructure of the U.S. homeland as well as for the international economic system, any future U.S. space deterrence concept must be tied into the homeland defense strategy of the United States. This fits with the present definition of homeland defense which is "the protection of United States sovereignty, territory, domestic population, and *critical infrastructure* against external threats and aggression."[217] [Emphasis added]

The Department of Defense states in doctrine that the United States will execute homeland defense "by detecting, deterring, preventing and defeating threats from actors of concern as far forward from the homeland as possible."[218] Space has been acknowledged in U.S. national strategies of the past to be one such vital "forward region" requiring coordination between services and agencies to ensure that the external threats do not impede the societal operations and the continued advancement of the protection of life and property.

---

216 Boyd, John. "Patterns of Conflict". Presentation, 1989. P. 8
217 Joint Publication 1-02 <u>DoD Dictionary of Military Terms</u>/ 2015
218 Joint Publication 3-27 <u>Homeland Defense</u>

To accomplish this, the *Strategy for Homeland Defense and Civil Support Joint Operating Concept* provides five mission layers to accomplish within the forward regions and should be the high level framework for protecting our homeland's space critical infrastructure and "ensuring the freedom of action, full access and use of capabilities…in space"[219] :

- Detection
- Deterrence
- Preventative Actions
- Defeating Threats
- "As Far Forward…as possible"[220]

First, the detection of threats in the forward region of space requires space situational awareness (SSA). As a mission area, the DoD has invested in SSA ground based sensors such as the Space Surveillance Telescope (SST), the C-Band radar, and the Space Fence. In addition, the Space Surveillance Network (SSN), originally designed to track space and missile threats to the United States from the Eisenhower years forward, has provided a catalogue of space objects for US Strategic Command's Joint Functional Component Command for Space (JFCC SPACE).[221] In 2014, the U.S. Air Force launched the newest space surveillance system called GSSAP (Geosynchronous Space Situational Awareness Program) to monitor the GEO orbital regime. While a good start, this is an area requiring much more fidelity and accuracy to ensure a robust understanding of space activities and potential threats to American space systems. How much fidelity and accuracy are required necessitates further analysis beyond the scope of this paper.

Second is deterrence, the main theme of this book and of the NSSS. While the NSSS is linked to the Strategy for Homeland Defense by the DoD, in practice there has not been much connectivity with this strategy just as there has been no real deterrence capability or capacity in the NSSS itself. It

---

219 Joint Publicans 3-27 Homeland Defense. Department of Defense. 2013. P. III-14

220 Department of Defense Homeland Defense and Civil Support Joint Operating Concept. Version 2.0. 1 Oct 2007. P. 19.

221 Spires, David N. Beyond Horizons: A Half Century of Air Force Space Leadership. Air Force Space Command. 2002. P. 187

is recommended that, for true deterrence to work as part of an overarching strategy for defense of American freedom of action[222] and population's access to our critical space infrastructure, that effective deterrence and protection, requires a layered capability for action, not rhetorical implements of perceived norm building. This concept of deterrence has been shown to be flawed given the present strategic reality and culture of the People's Republic of China's view of space warfare. This will be covered in more detail later in this chapter.

Third is preventative action. This is essentially taking the Chinese concept of "attack to deter" and applying it to the U.S. homeland defense of space capabilities. Given the aforementioned offensive dominant nature of the space forward region, and the difficulty if not near impossibility of actively protecting space assets from attack, especially kinetic attacks, self-defense may require a preventative attack against the Chinese "mobile warfare" space assets such as their KE ASAT systems. Should indications and warnings from our overhead reconnaissance satellites, aircraft, or SSA sensors indicate that ground-based space attack assets are posturing to leave their bases, a preventative strike on those mobile KE ASATs may be the only sure means of defending the homeland's critical space infrastructure.

As reversible means of counterspace activities such as jamming may already have been targeting our space systems in various orbital regimes, this type of preventative, and limited set of strikes should be viewed as a counterstrike and not a first-strike. The goal of this would be gaining escalation dominance over the situation to put the United States and its allied partners in a better position to dictate terms and to achieve the objectives of the next level of homeland defense strategy: defeating threats.

Defeating threats is the fourth level of the present homeland defense strategy and doctrines within the forward regions and the approaches. This requires capabilities and the political will to engage and defeat the threat as far away as possible from the United States and as stated in the Strategy for Homeland Defense of 2013. Space is much further from the homeland in many cases than engagements in the air domain or cyber domains. However, it must be recognized and remembered that for centuries, international law recognized that nations need not suffer an attack before they can lawfully take action to defend

---

222 Freedom of action in space is a principle held by the United States since the early days of the Space Age. It refers to the ability to freely access and execute operations of varying types (military, civil, commercial), without harmful interference or prevention and/or negation of those actions in space.

themselves against forces that present an imminent danger of attack.[223] This was the reason behind the Eisenhower Administration's directive to create our overhead reconnaissance satellites to assure the ability to prevent surprise attack against the forces or people of the United States in Pearl Harbor-style attack.[224] The build-up of adversary space forces should be no different.

The United States must adapt the concept of imminent threat to the capabilities and objectives of today's potential adversaries such as China, who do not seek in the near term to attack us using conventional means. Instead, Chinese strategic and military planners rely on asymmetric means to strike at the US homeland's space-enabled diplomatic, economic and information instruments of power, thus limiting the effectiveness of the U.S. force projection from US bases into the Western Pacific. Their space weapons, terrestrially-based, kinetic and non-kinetic, can be used in various permutations without warning and without following a specific method of escalation such as from reversible means to kinetic - it could be all out kinetic strikes without any indications of reversible purposeful interference.

This long-held option of preventative attack is needed in order to defeat threats to American and allied space systems linked to the homeland and our civil and military operations worldwide. The magnitude of this growing threat and its link to the homeland make it more compelling than in the past when commanders had other priorities in other operating domains following the early Space Age and space systems had yet to prove their mission utilities to a broader audience than nuclear deterrence support.

Given the interdependent nature of our space infrastructure with other vital areas of American critical infrastructure such as energy, commerce and financial markets, even if uncertainty remains as to the time and place of an adversary attack on space or related ground components, the U.S. should keep options open to act preventatively to defeat the attack while in the forward regions and not afterwards.[225] The present day language of "fighting through"

---

223 Paraphrased from the 2002 National Security Strategy and applied to the 21st Century space environment

224 Terrill, Delbert A. The Air Force Role in Developing International Outer Space Law. Air University Press. May 1999. p. 4

225 Paraphrased and updated from the 2002 National Security Strategy view on pre-emption as means to defeat attacks against the homeland. Edited for current space environment and ASAT threats.

and absorbing attacks will detract, not enhance, deterrence or American leadership in providing "a safe, operating environment...to enhance trade and exploration."[226] Threats of attack must be defeated prior to the mobile warfare pieces are moved out of a visible, targetable location, otherwise, the final aspect of homeland defense doctrine, "as far forward as possible," will become a lost opportunity in the event of a crisis erupting.[227]

## Counter-Strategy Part 2: Escalation Dominance-Based Space Deterrence[228]

Given the analysis of the strategic culture of China, warfighting doctrines, and space force developments and deployments as part of their overarching counter-intervention strategy in the Pacific, American strategists should create a national security space strategy that supports and acknowledges the strategy of homeland defense and the core interests of the United States in the Pacific. To do this requires shaping the capabilities and support infrastructure into an operational framework capable of providing the President with the capabilities needed to address each of the potential types of deterrence scenarios required. Adapting Herman Kahn's tiered approach to deterrence, this framework includes three Tiers: Tier 1 Deterrence, Tier II Deterrence and Tier III Deterrence.

Tier 1 Deterrence addresses the Chinese view of a nuclear-spacepower nexus they term "strategic deterrence." The survival of the CCP and the PLA in the context of their space enabled counter-intervention strategy creates an escalation dominance effect should the United States not create a capability to create friction in Chinese planning. This requires publically declaring that the

---

226 Dolman, Everett. Astropolitik: Classical Geopolitics in the Space Age. Frank Cass. 2002. P. 157

227 Keep in mind that according to Chinese analysts, the Chinese have in the past been willing to create a crisis by using force to achieve their policy objectives. RAND's study on *Chinese Patterns of the Use of Force* in 1999 highlighted examples of this and showcased how the Chinese term for crisis has a mixed meaning of opportunity and danger.

228 Escalation dominance is defined by the RAND Corporation's Dangerous Thresholds p. 15 as: "a condition in which a combatant has the ability to escalate a conflict in ways that will be disadvantageous or costly to the adversary while the adversary cannot do the same in return, either because it has no escalation options or because the available options would not improve the adversary's situation."

United States will not tolerate interference or attacks upon systems supporting US nuclear command and control, will be considered escalatory, threatening stability between the two nations and the survival of the U.S. homeland, supporting critical infrastructure and populations. This will require the posturing of American space forces forward from terrestrial launching sites at sea and in the air, as well as posturing of nuclear forces as a strategic communication to Beijing as a means to achieve policy change objectives.

Tier II Deterrence addresses the buildup of Chinese terrestrial and orbital counterspace forces to threaten the US space infrastructure ground and space segments. This deterrence requires a multi-layered counterspace portfolio capable of providing the President with multiple options to include preventative attacks on adversary ASAT garrisons, directed energy weapons as well as Chinese space based ISR and communications capabilities. The goal of these strikes would be to achieve a limited war aim of self-defense of U.S. space systems and the protection of the means of 21st Century American society and instruments of national power. In addition, it could also support a larger aim such as the creation of friction, uncertainty, and disunity in Chinese command and control within the mainland and throughout the Pacific region.

This requires the development and deployment of a survivable triad of capabilities utilizing a joint or allied combined force concept on land, air, and sea[229]. On land and sea, a modified version of the Aegis/Standard Missile-3 missile defense system could be deployed in a ring around the Western Pacific island chains from Alaska down through Australia and India. Coupled with sensors already in theater, with those launched into GEO for SSA, these weapons have the capability of not only achieving a LEO or a Medium Earth Orbit (MEO) ASAT capability against potential adversary ISR assets, but could also provide a notional space reconstitution denial system at mid-course altitudes. Finally, these systems could provide a means to defend US assets against terrestrially-launched ASAT missiles fired from deployed "mobile warfare" locations. Table 1 highlights these attitude regimes of the SM-3.[230]

---

229 This triad of capabilities for space warfighting and defense is not to be confused with the nuclear triad of bombers, submarines and ballistic missiles. This is strictly terrestrial based space forces.

230 www.allthingsnuclear.com

| SM-3 Variant | Estimated SM-3 maximum reachable altitudes | |
| --- | --- | --- |
| | Burnout Velocity in (km/s) | Maximum Reachable Altitude (km) |
| Block 1A | 1052 | 1952 |
| Block IIA (lower range) | 1080 | 2025 |
| Block IIA (upper range) | 1095 | 2175 |

Finally, the sea and land-based legs of the counterspace triad includes air-launched ASAT capabilities that can be based overseas or at home as part of a new global space sovereignty alert force, capable of engaging targets in all orbital planes and at varying altitudes. The technology for this is also available through several research and development programs going back decades such as the successfully tested Celestial Eagle concept, as well as DARPA's current Airborne Launch Assist Space Access (ALASA) program. ALASA is a program dedicated to providing a low-cost means to get satellites into orbit and as such could serve as an ASAT platform as well as an operationally responsive, low cost reconstitution method for some mission areas and orbital altitudes. The ability to relocate and launch quickly from virtually any major runway around the world substantially reduces the time needed to launch a mission. Launching from an aircraft provides launch point offset, which permits essentially any orbit direction to be achieved without concerns for launch direction limits imposed by geography at fixed-base launch facilities.[231]

Tier III Deterrence would require only reversible counter-action leveraging the purposeful interference norm of behavior as deterrence or retribution to terrestrial actions or actions against space segment assets. This would

231 Clapp, Mitchell Burnside. Airborne Launch Assist Space Access Fact Sheet. http://www. darpa.mil/program/airborne-launch-assist-space-access

require a series of capabilities to negate signals or types of signals in an entire channel, sets of channels, an entire transponder, sets of transponders, the entire satellite, the entire constellation of a certain satellite type, all satellites flagged by the adversary, or all satellites--regardless of registry--that are suspected of aiding the adversary in its counter-intervention strategy. This would provide a debris-free alternative, provided of course that the adversary does not see the benefits of escalation to kinetic exchanges for a combined countervalue/counterforce strike. This provides a potential for deterrence through the threat of "soft kill" against adversary capabilities to target the Pacific Fleet, disrupt effective command and control of U.S. and Allied forces and create lower levels of escalation dominance to achieve policy objectives and ensure access to space capabilities and benefits for the homeland [the defense of the homeland's space dependent way of life].

Each of these tiers would require a tailored approach given the different potential adversaries. In the case of China, a more aggressive approach based on escalation dominance would take the Chinese decision cycle and invert it in the favor of the United States and its allies. To ensure that a decision loop is conducted in sufficiently rapid manner with enough variety in capabilities and response types to maintain uncertainty and unpredictability in the minds of the adversary, a decision tool is required for strategists and commanders to enable them to decide what course of action the adversary patterns are highlighting, how to stay ahead of their decision calculus, and how to effectively confuse and paralyze it. One method is through a space warfare escalation ladder as depicted in list below:

Non-Interference/Peaceful Use of Space

1. Freedom of Action in Space (civil, commercial, military use of space for benefit of nation and world)
2. Intelligence/SSA Collections (Passive/Active)

Reversible, Yet Purposeful Interference Threshold (Deny/Degrade)

3. Passive Jamming
4. Active Jamming/Cyber Attacks
5. Laser Tracking/Dazzling

6. Unauthorized, Rendezvous and Proximity Operations Near U.S. or allied spacecraft
7. Posturing/Mobilization of Destructive Space Attack Forces

Irreversible, Purposeful Interference Threshold (Damage)

8. High Energy Chemical Laser
9. High Power Microwave Weapons Use

Kinetic, Debris Generation Threshold (Destroy)

10. Kinetic Energy (KE) Anti-Satellite (ASAT) missiles (Terrestrial Based-LEO)
11. Kinetic Energy (KE) Anti-Satellite (ASAT) weapons (Co-Orbital)
12. Kinetic Energy (KE) Anti-Satellite (ASAT) missiles (Terrestrial Based-GEO)

Nuclear Use Threshold (Destroy)

13. Terrestrial Fractional Orbital Bombardment Systems (FOBS)
14. Orbital Electro-Magnetic Pulse (EMP)
15. Orbital Nuclear Strike against spacecraft (all orbital regimes affected)

As with Herman Kahn's escalation ladder of nuclear warfare, this space escalation ladder is intended to serve as a tool for decision makers to assess the situation and stay ahead of the adversary decision calculus by observing the patterns of strategic and operational behavior, and re-orienting the U.S. space and terrestrial forces to be rapidly capable of escalating into a position that prevents the destruction of critical space systems and the economic and information instruments of power. This proposed tool is not all encompassing and provides only a few examples of adversary actions within each threshold to provide context. Also, it is important to note that just because this shows a step by step method of escalating space engagements from peacetime to total war, an adversary is not limited to starting with reversible means and staying there or gradually escalating. Indeed, as the Chinese way of offensive space deterrence highlights, depending on the decision calculus and the perceived level of opportunity or danger in a given situation, PLA space forces could very well conduct an offensive combining several thresholds or going direct to destructive, rapid attack postures to achieve their policy and military objectives.

The first threshold is that of the ideal peacetime condition the present DoD Space Policy promotes which is non-interference or peaceful use of space. This describes conditions intended by the international space legal regimes such as freedom of action in space for civil space exploration, commercial space development, and military uses of space for the national and multinational interest. In addition, it also includes military operations such as intelligence and space situational awareness operations to assure the status quo is maintained by all spacefaring nations.

Once a state such as China crossed the threshold of reversible, yet purposeful interference, the escalatory requirements for observing the jamming, laser tracking, or dazzling type behavior would require sufficient, rapid response from U.S. leadership and commanders to achieve a higher level of escalation through a combination of offensive and defensive capabilities as well as uncertainty generated in the minds of the adversary. Once an adversary continues up the patterns and trends of potential denial and degradation of U.S. space systems, U.S. leaders can choose to allow the adversary to continue to deny and degrade our systems or to escalate the ladder to a higher level to prevent further denial or a rapid escalation to the next threshold which is described as the kinetic, debris generation threshold.

Once the kinetic threshold has been crossed, destruction of U.S. space assets are the adversary's clear objective within their destructive space warfare concept.. This could be terrestrially-based ASAT attacks, or space-based co-orbital ASATs, and directed energy weapons such as high power microwave and lasers. As the situation escalates, the maximum damage that could be done is a more extreme scenario where the adversary decides to destroy all threats to its national survival by detonating nuclear weapons in space to deny the benefits of space and create severe havoc to the strategic space COG of the United States and its allies and space partners.

## Conclusions

The vulnerability of American and allied space systems by the Chinese's rapidly developing counterspace forces presents a major threat to the homeland as well as to American forward presence and influence in the Pacific. As a result, it is key to understand that in addition to being force multipliers for American force projection worldwide, spacepower is also intertwined in every layer of U.S. critical infrastructure including energy, transportation, finance, and information flow, placing the civil population and the American way of life at risk. Thus, it is imperative that the United States remove the vulnerability and actively sustain our space infrastructure while providing the means to deter Chinese aggression in the Pacific. This requires the inversion of the Tao and moving friction and vulnerability from our side, to China by utilization of Eastern deterrence methods and an escalation dominance based deterrence construct. The National Security Space Strategy's space deterrence concept does not fulfill this vital task for the defense of the homeland and its freedom of action in space.

The inadequacy of the present NSSS approach to space deterrence that this book has reviewed has become a concern within the halls of Congress as well as some sectors of academia. In 2012, the late RAND strategist Therese Delpech, known best for her work on nuclear deterrence theory, wrote:

> "The United States is in a unique position because of its intensive and extensive use of space-based systems…It possesses known asymmetrical advantages in space and information technologies, but its superiority is associated with a major weakness: the vulnerability of its space…assets to attacks…How it can secure its space advantage for its own sake and that if its allies is one of the most important security questions [of] the beginning of the 21st Century."[232]

The United States Congress, in the FY15 National Defense Authorization Act (NDAA), Section 1606, recognized that given the evolving and increasing threats to U.S. space systems and the critical infrastructure of the nation by China and other states, the DoD should re-think its NSSS space deterrence concept and force posture in order to achieve an "effective deterrence posture" through "space superiority." This book has covered options related to many Congressional mandated requirements which include offensive space operations and the active protection of national security space assets.[233]

---

232 Delpech, Therese. <u>Nuclear Deterrence in the 21st Century</u>. RAND. 2012. P. 144
233 FY15 National Defense Authorization Act, Section 1606, Update of National Security Space Strategy to Include Space Control and Space Superiority Strategy

While some analysts believe that promoting such a strategy of a tiered, tailored, triad of offensive, terrestrial based capabilities to be destabilizing, the facts indicate that the lack of these actions to provide active protection capabilities to the United States is in truth the real destabilizing factor. First strike stability, escalation decision ladders, and deterrence all must be re-invented, given the offense dominant nature of space and the destabilizing nature of the Chinese advantage maintained in all three areas over the United States.[234] This book has attempted to begin this discussion toward a strategy that utilizes current industrial capacity, programs of record, and is consistent with the legal obligations of the Outer Space Treaty. Basing the protection of a vital COG of the American way of life, economic power and military effectiveness on vulnerability and passivity will lead to "ruin."[235] The time for allowing states and non-state actors to purposefully interfere and threaten our critical space infrastructure with kinetic and non-kinetic first strike should end. A more aggressive and serious approach is called for given the security needs of our time. Surprise attacks could occur in a matter minutes, and countering this trend will not be easy, particularly since a reliable deterrence strategy has not been publically articulated due to the risk of a crisis in space escalating out of control. The risk of escalation, as in the Cold War nuclear standoff, has always been present in the past, but in the case of space attacks, in an offensive dominant domain, is a different kind of risk. However, as Therese Delpech stated with regard to this issue of space deterrence, "deterrence by threat of punishment remains the best available strategy for the most serious threats."[236]

---

234 Delpech, Therese. Nuclear Deterrence in the 21st Century. RAND. 2012. P. 143
235 Ibid. p. 147
236 Ibid. p. 147

# References

Boyd, John. "Patterns of Conflict". Presentation. 1989

Boyd, John. "Organic Design of Command and Control." Presentation. 1990

Beilenson, Laurence W. The Treaty Trap. Public Affairs Press. 1969

Brodie, Bernard. Strategy in the Missile Age. RAND. 2007

Burles, Mark. Patterns in China's Use of Force: Evidence from History and Doctrinal Writings. RAND, 2000.

Cheng, Julie. "Confucianism and WMD.: Ethics and Weapons of Mass Destruction. Cambridge Press. 2004

Cheng, Dean. "Chinese View of Deterrence". Joint Forces Quarterly Fourth Quarter, 2011

"China Military Aims to Build Up Space Defences" Sky News Online. 15 Apr 2014. http://news.sky.com/story/1242772/china-military-aims-to-build-up-space-defences

Clapp, Mitchell Burnside. Airborne Launch Assist Space Access Fact Sheet. Accessed August 20, 2015. http://www.darpa.mil/program/airborne-launch-assist-space-access, undated.

Department of Defense Homeland Defense and Civil Support Joint Operating Concept. Version 2.0. 1 Oct 07

Department of Defense: Military and Security Developments Involving the People's Republic of China, 2015

DeBlois, Bruce. "Space Sanctuary: A Viable National Strategy. *Air and Space Power Journal*. Winter 1998

De Selding, Peter B. "Eutelsat Blames Ethiopia as Jamming Incidents Triple." Space News. June 6, 2014

Delpech, Thérèse. Nuclear Deterrence in the 21st Century. RAND. 2012

Dolman, Everett. Astropolitik: Classical Geopolitics in the Space Age. Frank Cass. 2002

Egan, Matthew Jude. "Anticipating Future Vulnerability: Defining Characteristics of Increasingly Critical Infrastructure-like Systems." Journal of Contingencies and Crisis Management. Vol 15, No 1. March 2007

Elder, Robert. From the Mind to the Feet.: Assessing the Perception-to-Intent-to-Action Dynamic. Air University. 2011.

Finch, Jay. "Bringing Space Crisis Stability Down to Earth." Joint Forces Quarterly 76, 1st Qtr, 2015

FY15 National Defense Authorization Act (NDAA), Section 1606: Update of National Security Space Strategy to include Space Control

Gompert, David C. "Mutual Restraint in Space". Paradox of Power: Sino-American Strategic Restraint in an Age of Vulnerability. National Defense University.2011

Harrison, Roger, et al. "The Delicate Balance of Risk": Space Deterrence Study. Eisenhower Center for Space and Defense Studies. United States Air Force Academy. 2010

Johnson-Freese, Joan. Space as a Strategic Asset. Columbia University Press. 2007

Joint Publication 1-02 Dictionary of Military Terms 2015. www.dtic.mil/doc-trine/new_pubs/**jp1_02**.pdf

Joint Publication 3-27 Homeland Defense 2013. www.dtic.mil/doctrine/new_pubs/**jp3_27**.pdf

Kahn, Herman, On Thermonuclear War. Princeton University Press. 1960

Kartchner, Kerry et al. Strategic Culture and Weapons of Mass Destruction: Culturally based Insights into Comparative National Security Policymaking. Palgrave-Macmillan. 2009

Kissinger, Henry. On China. Penguin Book. 2011

Kuznar, Lawrence. From the Mind to the Feet: Assessing the Perception-To-Intent-To-Action Dynamic. Air University Press. 2011

Li Hechun. "Sky War – A New form of War That Might Erupt in the Future," Liberation Army Daily, 17 January 2001

Lee, James G, Counterspace Operations for Information Dominance .Air University Press, 1995

Marquez, Peter. "Space Deterrence: The Pret a Porter Suit for the Naked Emperor," in Robert Butterworth, et. al., Marshall Institute. 2011

Marquez, Peter. Interview. 2014

Meek, Philip. "Testimony before the U.S. –China Economic and Security Review Commission Hearing: China's View of Sovereignty and Methods of Access Control.". February 27, 2008

Mehnken, Thomas G. "Secrecy and Stratagem: Understanding Chinese Strategic Culture." Lowy Institute for International Policy, Sydney, Australia. Feb 2011

MacDonald, Bruce W. China, Space Weapons and U.S. Security. CFR Press. 2008

MacDonald, Bruce W, "Testimony before the Strategic Forces Subcommittee, House Armed Forces Committee," March 18, 2009

Morgan, Forrest, Deterrence and First Strike Stability in Space. RAND, 2010

Nayobi, Nima. "Geosynchronous Orbit and the Outer Limits of Westphalian Sovereignty." Hastings Science & Technology Law Journal, Vol. 3, p. 471, Summer 2011

Nisbett, Richard. The Geography of Thought: How Asians and Westerners Think Differently and Why. Free Press. New York. 2003

Payne, Keith. The Great American Gamble. National Institute for Public Policy Press. 2008.

Payne, Keith. The Fallacies of Cold War Deterrence. National Institute for Public Policy Press. 2001

Pollpeter, Kevin. China Dream, Space Dream: A Report Prepared for the U.S.-China Economic and Security Commission. IGCC. 2014

Qing Cao, "Selling culture: ancient Chinese conceptions of 'the other' in legends," The Zen of International Relations: IR Theories from East to West, ed. S. Chan. Basingstoke & New York. 2001

Richardson, Derek. The Rise of the Dualistic Dragon: Contrastive Strategic Mentality of the People's Republic of China Under American Hegemonism. University of Victoria. 2008

Rumsfeld, Donald et al. Report of the Commission to Assess United States National Security Space Management and Organization. 2001.

"Resiliency and Disaggregated Space Architectures." Air Force Space Command White Paper. 2013

Schelling, Thomas. Arms and Influence. Yale University Press, 1966

Schulte, Gregory. "Protecting Global Security in Space," Presentation at the S. Rajaratnam School of International Studies. Nanyang Technological University, Singapore May 9, 2012

Schulte, Gregory, and Audrey M. Schaffer. "Enhancing Security Through Responsible Use of Space." Strategic Studies Quarterly. Spring 2012.

Schulte, Gregory. "China and the New National Security Space Strategy". A Presentation to the U.S.-China Economic and Security Review Commission. May 11, 2011.

Schneider, Barry. Tailored Deterrence: Influencing States and Actors of Concern. USAF Counter Proliferation Center. 2011

Scobell, Andrew. China and Strategic Culture. Strategic Studies Institute. 2002

Secretary of Defense and the Director of National Intelligence, National Security Space Strategy. Department of Defense. 2011

Sun Zhaoli. Science of Strategy. Academy of Military Science Military Strategy Studies Dept. Beijing: Military Science Press, 2008

Sun Zhaoli. Science of Strategy. Academy of Military Science Military Strategy Studies Dept. Beijing: Military Science Press, December 2013

Sun Tzu. The Art of War. Shambhala Dragon Edition. Boston. 1988.

Tanner, Scott. China's Emerging National Security Interests and their Impact on the People's Liberation Army. Marine Corps University. 2015.

Tellis, Ashley. "China's Military Space Strategy." Survival. September 2007

Teng Jianqun, "Thoughts Arising from The U.S. Military's Space War Exercise," Liberation Army Daily, February 7, 2001, in Foreign Broadcast Information Service as "Jiefangjun Bao Views U.S. Preparations for Space Warfare," February 7, 2001

Terrill, Delbert R. The Air Force Role in Developing International Outer Space Law. Air University Press. May 1999.

United Nations. Treaty on Principles Governing the Activities of States in the Exploration and Use of Outer Space, including the Moon and Other Celestial Bodies. 1967

U.S. Department of Transportation National Transportation Systems Center. Global Positioning System Timing Signal Criticality Update. Report from the National Transportation Systems Center for the US Department of Transportation. July 2008

U.S. Department of Transportation. Vulnerability of the Transportation System Reliance on the Global Positioning System. Report from the National Transportation Systems Center. August 29, 2001

Warden, John A., III, Colonel, USAF, "The Enemy as a System". Airpower Journal. Spring 1995

Wholstetter, Roberta. Pearl Harbor: Warning and Decision. Stanford University Press. 1962. P. vii

Weeden, Brian et al. "An Introduction to Ostrom's Eight Principles for Sustainable Governance of Common-Pool Resources as a Possible Framework for Sustainable Governance in Space."

Weeden, Brian. "Protecting Space Assets through Denial Deterrence." Secure World Foundation Presentation. http://swfound.org/resource-library/publications/2008/12/protecting-space-assets-through-denial-deterrence/.

White House, National Space Policy of the United States of America. June 2010

Wortzel, Larry. The Dragon Extends Its Reach. Potomac Books. 2013

Xi, Jinping. "The Rejuvenation of the Chinese Nation is a Dream Shared by All Chinese". The Governance of China. Foreign Languages Press. Beijing. 2015